SOMETHING'S WRONG WITH AMERICA

I0442078

An Essay by an Optimistic Pessimist

Self-Published by

Paul B. Azodo

A non-politically correct look at current issues facing the United States of

America

COPYRIGHT

In loving memories of my Uncles Alex and Charles without whom I couldn't predict where I would be at this time in my life.

Contents

PREFACE

For several decades now, the United States appeared to be shifting away from whatever it had done in the past that brought it to the position of the most advanced nation in the world. It took her over 200 years to get there. But within the past few decades the country seemed to be drifting off course nudged along by cultural changes that some see as progress towards the future, while others see as sign of decline. There appear to be an impasse as to who is right and who is wrong since both sides seem pretty passionate about what they believe.

That is where the author comes in. As an immigrant in his 60's he does have the perspective of someone who is outside and looking in. He has watched the country from afar from his teenage years and has watched it up close too, having lived here for over 39 years. He remembers that the country used to have standards by which performance was measured, whether in school or at the workplace. He remembers when the trophy receivers were only those who performed well. He remembers that society used to have dos and don'ts and good and bad. He remembers when the two words, "politically correct" were not in American-English vocabulary.

Today, the times have changed, and so did the direction of the society. Nobody knows where the country is going to end up and what that end is going to look like. For now, people appear to be only interested in winning the day and let the future take care of itself. Yet, children are being born every day that may be the ones to experience what the future is going to bring.

We have just had an election that was the first of its kind in the history of this country because many believed that it was won as a result of indirect bribery of voters, whether the implicit bribery was in the form of welfare benefits or amnesty for illegal immigrants. Whatever people in either side believe, the American political system has been shot in the leg, and it is going to be limping along for a long time until it figures out how to cure itself.

The author is not a political pundit but an ordinary citizen, with no party affiliation, who has always been interested in history and current affairs. He likes to observe things around him. He also believes that political correctness may pat some in the back but will eventually destroy the society, because it is in the way of truth and honest discussion of the issues facing society. It is from this point of view that this book approaches what the author sees happening to this country, and hopes that the reader can squeeze a moment in the racy world that we live in to honestly reflect on some of the issues discussed in this book. The author is under no illusion that he is going to change the world but just wants to add his voice to those already out there, in the wilderness.

1. MY PHILOSOPHY

I am a pessimist but I am optimistic in my pessimism, which makes me a balanced person; in other words, I cannot be accused of being unbalanced in my views. As a balanced person, I am able to look inside myself to understand what kind of a person I am, my strengths, weaknesses, abilities, and inabilities. I am able to think about all the things I wish I could do or be but couldn't. I am able to identify the reasons why I am unable to be or do those things that I wished I could have been or done. My conclusion is that we are unable to be or do all the things we wish we could be or do as a result of the limitations nature put in all human beings. I consider this ability to search inside and understand myself very important because it allows me to coexist peacefully with others regardless of who they are and what their stations are in life. It allows me to admire those who have the natural gift to do those things that did not come naturally to me and learn from them. It also allows me to understand and respect those that are unable to do things that seem natural to me. Understanding who I am and what my capabilities are has enabled me to avoid a life of frustration, resentment, and hatred of others that I might perceive as doing or being better than I am. A wise expression I heard growing up in Nigeria says that: "If you don't know who is bigger than you are, you probably don't know who is smaller than you are." What the expression does is teach us to be able to learn from those who know better than us and also be able to teach those who know less than us. If we become envious of those who know or do better than us and seek to destroy them, they will probably die off with their knowledge and skill. The world would not be better off if that happens. Perhaps, it explains why human beings don't keep others that are more knowledgeable than they are in slavery for long. They soon give the enslaved their freedom, so that they can help solve the day to day problems for the benefits of all.

Looking at life in a balance way allows me to enjoy where I am or where I live at the moment. I am able to remind myself of why I left the place I was born, which allows me to appreciate the country that I now call my home. One of the ways of appreciating my new home is to promise myself that I will always do my best to contribute to making it better or, at least, make sure that I do not contribute to making it any worse than it was when I came. After all, if my old home was as good as my new home, and provided me with the kind of life I wished to have, there would have been no reason for me to seek a new home. Based on this, I find it irrational for anyone who immigrated to the United States for a better life to try and recreate here the society that he left behind. Coming to the United States as an adult was an advantage for me because it enabled me to keep the good aspects of the culture of the society I grew up in while adopting the aspects of American culture that I consider to be positive. If a majority of immigrants to the United States can adopt this principle, immigrants will make lasting positive contributions to this country, and immigration will not be just a source of cheap labor and large number of consumers of goods but also a source of revitalization for America. The enormous political, social, and economic problems now facing the United States may be blamed on lack of philosophical approach to issues important to society. We seem to have lost the ability to try and think about the reasons why we do things and what will be the immediate as well as the long term consequences of our actions.

I have degrees in agricultural and mechanical engineering but I have always considered myself a philosophical person in the sense that I always try to go beyond what things and situations are and consider the reasons for their being so, their roots, what would be the results if the situation is reversed. Would they be the same, better, or worse? I was already in high school when I first realized that people can make up stories about incidents that never took place, and make them sound believable. I don't pretend to be smarter than the average person out there, but I am able to rid myself of frustration, envy, anger, and resentment of others because of my station in life. I am not perfect but something inside always reminds me of who I am and who I continue to aspire to be, and to take myself seriously. When I raised my right hand before a judge at my citizenship ceremony to swear an oath to defend the constitution and the flag of the United States and uphold the law, I took the oath seriously. As I stepped out of the court room, I was aware that I was stepping out then as an American. From then on, I was only going to refer to the United States as my home in my mind and in conversation with others. In fact, from that day on, if my country of birth were to face off with the United States in a soccer match, I would be rooting for the American team. I believe that people who do not take oaths seriously are likely to disobey the law when nobody is watching. They are also the types that do not live up to contracts or take treaties seriously.

As I listen to the arguments now raging in this country on political and social issues, which have almost now split this country into two irreconcilable ideological camps, I wonder why, with all the "intelligent" people in this country, nobody seems to be asking the fundamental questions. These fundamental questions should be asked and honestly debated if we can ever stop ourselves dead on the track that is now leading us into the abyss. Do successful or rich people really prevent the middle class or poor people from being who they wish to be in life or are middle class and poor people restricted by nature to where they are in life? Is it common for intelligent and hardworking people of any race to fail in pursuit of what they like to do? It seems to me that being unable to point finger at the ghost of nature, we are turning the fingers on one another, thereby generating conflicts where there should be none. Somehow, we manage to find reasons to justify human conflicts that may end up destroying all of us.

The world will become better when we learn to live a balanced life. Then we will not do too little or too much of anything. We will be able to not only let others know when they do something wrong but also praise them when they do something right. When we decide or set out to correct past injustice, we should be careful not to swing too far to the other side and end up perpetuating the same injustice that we set out to correct. We shouldn't do the same thing for which we condemn others. People who need help should receive it but the giver should insist that the receiver abandon any behaviors that contribute to the bad situation, and make effort to become better. As we expect the gifted, the rich, and the successful to be conscientious about helping the poor and needy, we must also expect the poor and needy to be conscientious about contributing to their own well being as much as they can. It is important that the poor is aware that those who are successful cannot be faulted for their station in life; after all, we all entered this life under the same condition - as helpless human beings. Maintaining a balance in our lives is probably the most important universal behavior that can bring peace to all human beings regardless of the society they live in.

2. MOTIVATION FOR THIS BOOK

This book may well be the obituary of a great but short-lived civilization, the United States of America. Prior to 2008 election, I held hope that America might stop and reverse its decline, but after Barack Hussein Obama was elected I was convinced that a nail has been driven on the coffin of the United States of America. Nonetheless, I still held a dim of hope that sometimes if you can't smell anything, you may have to taste both water and alcohol to differentiate them, if they are similarly packaged. I thought that four years would have given Americans enough time to wake up and say "once bitten, twice shy." American voters of all stripes, young, old, native born, and immigrants, had four whole years to know, hear, and read what they didn't get a chance to know, hear, and read before voting for Obama in 2008. No American president has ever made such a subject of so much post-election investigation and exposé in the history of this country. There were investigative reports, books, and documentaries all trying to let the American people know who they had elected into the office of the president of the United States of America.

The pursuit of information to peel off the mask and discover the real Barack Obama, behind all the flowery speeches, was particularly tedious because it involved three continents that are culturally miles apart: United States, Asia, and Africa, plus Hawaii, which is not in the continental United States, and whose culture fits somewhere between the first and third world. What was the reason for the intense effort to discover who Barack Obama really is? Barack Obama was not vetted the same way all past American presidential candidates have been vetted: from birth certificate, family history, schools attended and records, military service, previous employment, public offices held, foreign travels, to personal associations. For someone with the kind of background that Obama came into the White House with, being born to a foreign father and an American mother that could not be described as a patriotic American, by any stroke of imagination, a rigorous vetting should have been a must to enable the American people to know who they were going to let into the White House. It would have been important for American people to know if Obama believes in and loves America enough to overlook his abnormal background, and trust him with the captainship of the American ship that has been battered by the wave of two simultaneous wars. Unbelievably, no such rationale prevailed in Obama's case. Why?

Complacency is the most important of the reasons. It is an attitude that develops over time in an affluent society and it is very hard to recognize or even accept because it is in the nature of human beings. In a free and affluent society, people are comfortable and relatively safe, so it becomes difficult for them to see or recognize danger. It is very difficult, if not impossible, for a complacent society to see itself as such because it has become a way of life. With that kind of attitude already in dominance, war weariness is always a click away because war becomes a distraction and an intrusion. Also, don't forget that political correctness has been practiced for decades by every segment of society, including the government, press, private sector, schools, and institutions of higher learning. With that, any attempt to vet the first black presidential candidate, especially one with an aura of exoticism, would raise enough emotional outcry of racism that could shake the very ground we walk on. But that would not have been the case if American press had not swung too far to the left and stayed there for decades now.

So, after four years of efforts to unveil the real Barack Hussein Obama to the American people, the nail on the coffin of the United States of America was not pulled out to try and resuscitate the country. Barack Hussein Obama was miraculously re-elected for another four years, for a total of eight years, so that he can continue with his quest for revenge against a people and a country he perceives as arrogant, unjust, bloated with greed, bullying, exploitative, militaristic, dismissive, and derisive of other people and countries. Obama's childhood experience has filled him with a great deal of frustration and resentment against the nation that he is now the president of. Without any doubt, he is now successfully getting the revenge that he had dreamt of from his teenage years without appearing to be doing so. With the active support of liberals in all walks of life, especially the social justice warrior cadre, Obama has now created opportunity for millions of people to live on government handouts and for millions of immigrants to bring in millions more relatives and friends to be dumped into taxpayers' care. America is now completely set up for the takedown. I imagine that it would take the United States 80 years to recover from eight years of Barack Obama's presidency, but I doubt very much that this country will ever recover intact from what Barack Obama has set in motion. It took this country over 200 years to become the greatest nation on earth but in just four years, an unknown character called Barack Hussein Obama has set it tumbling downhill.

There is no doubt that there were people who assured themselves that giving Obama the benefit of the doubt for four years, just to see how things would turn out wouldn't hurt anything, because no politician can destroy a country like the United States in just four years. Unfortunately, many of these people in their haste to experiment with the first black American president did not bother to pay attention to warning that Obama may have spent his years in college studying all the radicals' theories of fundamentally transforming a society like the United States. It turned out to be a piece of cake for Obama and his radical progressive partners; all it took was to convince the so-called poor and middle class that the successful Americans have been exploiting them, and that they have not been getting a fair share of the national pie as they had previously thought. If you have never looked inside to figure out who you are and what your capabilities are, and why you are not like the people you admire or envy, then you are likely easy to be convinced that someone else is responsible for keeping you from having all the good things that you see others enjoying. That was what happened when Obama showed up and finally convinced the so-called poor and middle class American voters that, he, Barack Hussein Obama, is the one that has been sent to right the wrong, and immediately set about pulling millions of Americans into the welfare system, regardless of whether they needed it or not, or whether they were qualified or not. That was all it took to set the fundamental transformation of the United States in motion. You have to be aware that a family classified as poor in the United States will most likely be equivalent to a middle class family elsewhere. It is naïve for anyone to think that Obama and his progressive cohorts are geniuses. Far from it; what they did to America was evil but wasn't any more difficult than taking a candy from a child literally, thanks to the complacent state of this society. Don't forget that it is easier to destroy things than to build them.

Some may continue to deceive themselves into believing that Obama is making America a better country, but the fact is that America is never going to return to its old glorious self. That was the goal of Barack Obama and his fellow radicals. Perhaps, it does not occur to many Americans that a lot of radicals have sadistic nature or evolved into sadists as a result of internalized frustrations and resentments. There is no evidence that the same young people that voted overwhelmingly for Obama have a notion of how Obama feels about young Americans and what his presidency means to the country in which they hope to live out the rest of their lives. By the time the country passes through all the series of experimentations by the United Nations, the name United States of America may only exist in history books. But you need not worry; after all, who says that human civilizations must have a happy ending? For a human civilization to have a happy ending, it shouldn't have any ending at all, which is impossible.

For now, the re-election of Barack Hussein Obama has convinced me that the nail that was driven into America's coffin by his first election may never be fully pulled out to allow the country to be resuscitated. It is painful to watch a country that has been an example as well as envy of others in the world to decline under domestic and external forces. The external forces came in the way of immigrants who were allowed into the society and nurtured to continue business as usual. Whether the people that live in this country know it or not, the foundation of the United States is now being destroyed by internal forces that have convinced themselves that they are just progressing to the next wrung in the ladder of American civilization. These forces believe that America will become better off if it abandons its morality and permits a society where anything goes regardless of how contradictory to nature a particular moral behavior may be. Also, blinded by an obscure global vision, these forces believe that reliable agreements and alliances could be contracted with global entities and organizations that they barely understand. It is possible that a combination of arrogance and ignorance has convinced domestic agents of decline that those outside forces they seek to align themselves with are incapable of harming America. This is a clear example of how a powerful and advanced nation can lose to a less advanced and less powerful nation or forces. Hopefully, those who participate in the organizations, movements, and actions that contribute to the decline of the United States would be honest and courageous enough to accept the role they played in the defining events of 2008 and 2012.

Much as I believe that America's decline is an inevitable fate of all civilizations, I couldn't help but express my view about what is happening to the country. I hope that by doing so, I might contribute to the many voices out there in the wilderness. There may even be a tiny chance of making some people aware of the issues, particularly those that might be inclined to take a second look. The 2012 election has acted as a catalyst for me to start putting pieces of my thoughts about what is going on in this country together in this book. This book is about my personal philosophy and observations and how they relate to the social and political issues currently reshaping the United States. I almost got started on the book after the general election of 2008 because I believed that historians may eventually pinpoint that election as the "final event" that marked the decline of the United States. I say final event because the circumstances and agents of decline within and outside the United States have been at work for decades.

You may want to know why I believe that 2008 is the defining date. Well, there are several reasons. First, assuming that Barack Hussein Obama's father was really a Kenyan student, who had never taken up a United States citizenship, and his mother, who was born in the United States disliked the country so much that she was always looking to marry a foreigner who would take her away from it, Obama would be the only president ever elected by a country anywhere in the world, rich, poor, developed or underdeveloped, with his kind of family history and background. Second, some would say that Obama's success in spite of coming from a broken family is what shows how great America is - a country where anybody can achieve anything regardless of his or her family background. That may be true but those people forget that the kind of family background that Obama came from usually inflicts a psychological wound, if not a total damage, to a child, which may follow him into adulthood and through the rest of his life. The evidence of psychological damage abounds in the stories Obama told about his life, in his behaviors, and in several of his speeches. Obama was known to tell his classmates in Hawaii stories about coming from a family of Indonesian or Kenyan rulers, and that he would return to one of those countries to become a ruler. How many American kids are known to make up this kind of story? When a person finds himself in certain environment where he or she feels deficient, he or she may compensate for this deficiency by making up this kind of story. It allows him or her to fit in. However, children from stable family background know exactly who they are, and are not likely to cook up this kind of story. Unfortunately, once a child starts out that way, it may become part of his or her life unless someone catches it early enough and gets help for the child. If not, the individual grows up believing that this behavior is the only way to get ahead, unless he or she pays a price sooner by being exposed.

Fortunately for Obama, he seemed to receive nothing but applause whenever he made untrue or exaggerated statements. Over time, he has become confident about his ability to say anything and get away with it, whether it is true or false, real or imagined. A few times that some reporters tried to challenge Obama on his lies, he tried to explain them away or simply brushed them off as just misstatements. The biggest danger is that there is a strong possibility that anybody who grows up the way Obama did may harbor resentment of the very society he lives in, and may camouflage his quest for revenge against the society. After all, his mother grew up resentful of her country too. His presumed Kenyan father did not have a successful life either, in spite of studying in Harvard. He ended up a habitual drunk driver and died in a drunk-driving accident in Kenya. Obama's "Uncle Frank" (Frank Marshall Davis), his mentor in Hawaii, was an avowed communist. So, from whom could Obama have inherited his love for the United States of America?

As the fate of America would have it, by the time people had started to scrutinize Obama's stories and speeches, the Democratic Party and the mainstream media had already committed themselves to seeing him elected, and had built a fortress around him. So much for a transparent presidency! Now Obama is surrounded by radicals some of whom have history of communists or communist sympathizers in their families. So, this period in the history of America may be appropriately labeled the period of revenge of radical offspring of communists and communist sympathizers. As radicals now taste America's blood, they may get blinded to the possibility of unintended consequences of their revolution or fundamental transformation of the United States, as Barack Obama coined it. They may pay a huge price for their unnecessary and unwarranted adventurous plan to fundamentally transform America by making it weak economically, militarily, and culturally unidentifiable. After all, products from experiments involving human society aren't the same as chemical experiments where you already know what products to expect when you mix specific chemicals together.

Third, a person who was running for the position of the president of the United States had all his records, including college, passport, and travels sealed, so that nobody would know exactly what kind of life he had led. This contradicts the requirement that any American applying for a job in a national security agency or company must go through a security clearance. Following employment, the individual must report his or her travel destinations abroad on a regular basis to maintain the clearance status. Also, the justice system of the United States allows a defense lawyer to use the family background of an accused criminal, during both trial and sentencing phases, to ask for leniency because it is believed that the family history of the accused may have contributed to his or her criminal behavior. It was strange; therefore, that nobody cared about the history of Obama's badly broken family in considering him for the presidency of the United States.

So many questions arose from what happened first in 2008 and then miraculously repeated in 2012. For example, why was it assumed that Obama was psychologically fit to be president without knowing and taking into account what he did while growing up and how he earned his college degrees, his political beliefs, and other social activities? Is it still reasonable to expect the mainstream media to be the watchful eyes and ears of the people? Could American voters ever become really well informed about issues that affect the economic health and security of this country? They have been implicitly made to believe that government will never be out of money to pay for welfare programs, no matter how many more millions of people get on the government welfare wagon. What was it that convinced his supporters that Obama was qualified to be the president of the United States? Was it his graduation from Harvard University? He wasn't the first black man to graduate from that institution; a lot of black Americans, black Africans, black Latinos, and black West Indians had studied in that institution throughout its history.

Was it his being appointed the president of Harvard Law Review? Other people had held that position throughout the history of that institution. Was it because he is of mixed races? Well, there were, perhaps, millions of Americans of mixed races in this country before Obama came along. Was it because of Obama's ability to sound like Rev. Martin Luther King Jr., a civil right icon that many Americans respect? Strangely enough, Obama hasn't quoted much from Martin Luther King Jr. because his agenda as well as approach on the issues facing society are quite different from the messages of Dr. King. Dr. King's message had the nobler goal of uniting Americans as one family. When he marched for civil rights, his followers were not encouraged to confront other Americans or destroy properties. On the contrary, Obama's goal was not only to divide Americans in order to win an election but he actually urged his supporters to vote for revenge, confront and get in the face of those on the other side of their political viewpoint. It seems that his goal was to raise an army comprising of resentful Blacks, Hispanics, the so-called poor and middle class, radical progressives, trade unionists, immigrants, and other welfare recipients to destroy America. The current generation seems to be moving backwards towards darker days from the positive and peaceful message of Dr. King.

Obama had really not exhibited any exceptional quality prior to being propped up to run for the presidency of the United States. Obama appear to be comfortable around people only when he is giving a speech using a teleprompter and had shied away from impromptu interviews. A person with excellent memory and quick thinking mind would have no problem giving impromptu interviews. Obama's habit of constant hesitation when he speaks does not show that he possess a quick mind. My conclusion, therefore, is that it was the hand of fate that was pulling on America to take the plunge. As the expression goes, "Whatever that is meant to go wrong will go wrong."

3. THE BIRTH OF AMERICA

The United States, like all countries in the Americas was discovered by a European explorer, and eventually became colonized by England. Other European explorers from Spain discovered various other countries in the Americas. Brazil was discovered by a Portuguese explorer and is the only Portuguese speaking country in South America; however, it is a subcontinent and its population is larger than those of all of its Spanish speaking neighbors put together. With a few exceptions, all the countries in the Americas share the same historical background, which is that the countries were inhabited by various Indian tribes before the arrival of the Europeans. Later, West Africans were brought to the new colonies, as slaves, from across the other side of the Atlantic Ocean, to do the hard work building the new world. The Pilgrims who left England and settled in the new colony did so for religious freedom because the official religion of England at that time did not allow them to worship as they believed, even though they all belonged to the same Christian faith.

The only difference between the United States and the other countries in the Americas was that its settlers came for religious freedom. There wasn't any special miracle that caused the English colony to succeed that the Spanish, French, and Portuguese settlements were left out of. Americans did not do anything to impede the countries of Latin America from copying or repeating exactly whatever they did to develop the United States to become the greatest nation on earth. As a matter of fact, any one of the Latin American countries could have been more advanced than the United States or Canada, if they knew how. Why then do the Hispanics think that they have the right to enter the United States illegally? What is the justification for vilifying Americans when they object to such unprovoked invasion? Americans were not responsible for the failure of Latin Americans to develop their countries and enjoy the good life they seek in the United States and elsewhere.

The fact that the countries of the Americas share the same history but not the same cultural behavior is, in fact, the main factor that separates United States and Canada on one hand and the Latin American countries on the other hand. If they had conscientiously reproduced the system of governance in the United States and Canada, perhaps, the countries of the Americas would have come close to true developmental equality. Mass illegal immigration would have been nonexistent. Who is to blame for the failure of Latin America to match the advance of American and Canadian societies? Is it the fault of Americans and Canadians or the people of Latin America themselves? I am sure that liberal academicians and the immigration activists may come up with tons of excuses to justify why the United States and Canada are at fault for what kept Latin America underdeveloped. I have no doubt that many Americans and Canadians would be interested to know what they are.

4. SLAVERY AND THE AMERICAS

Slavery was part of the history of the human race; every society, regardless of its size, had practiced it for all kinds of reasons that included economics, spoil of war, and even religion. It was so pervasive that even people who were former slaves had been known to turn around and own slaves themselves. Even today as we speak, there may be some unfortunate people being held somewhere in the world against their will. The English philosopher, Thomas Hobbes, believed that man is always in a state of nature, which means that man has the tendency to hurt or kill others, but since nobody wants to be killed, people get together and make rules or laws to protect us from one another. The getting together is what we now call a society. It does not appear that the tendency in humans to hurt or kill one another has waned since Hobbes put forth his philosophy. On the contrary, every society now has volumes of law books that you can literally stack up to heaven. Those laws and rules are not made for the other animals that inhabit the earth with us; they are designed to control the behaviors of human beings. Human civilization is really a journey through the unknown along a winding path that sometimes recoils on itself. With the development and proliferation of weapons of mass destruction, it is uncertain that humans will ever get to the goal of their civilization, the utopian world, where we have all learned to discard bad experiences and only pass on the good ones.

European explorers to the African continent and the Americas did not have slavery in mind when they first set sail. However, as Europeans began to settle the Americas, economic necessity kindled the desire to find somebody with the capacity to do the hard work in the plantations and survive. They had become aware of clan and tribal wars in Africa where those captured were either sacrificed to the gods or kept as slaves. The concept of prisoner exchange did not exist during the tribal wars. I imagined that initially, the Europeans may have seen no harm in taking the slaves away from their captors to provide help in their explorations or put them to work in the Americas. They had attempted to use the Indians in the Americas for slave labor with disastrous consequences. The Indians were dying in large numbers because of the hardship to which they were subjected. That prompted the Pope to issue a decree forbidding the European colonialists from using the natives for slave labor. The Pope, however, did not issue such a decree forbidding the colonialists from using Africans for slave labor, an omission that has never been explained by the Church.

It was said that an African slave could do work that would require about four Indians in the plantation, and that the Africans did not succumb to disease easily as the Indians. That may have contributed to the Pope's omission of African slaves in his decree. I have also speculated that since very little was known about the black race at the time of slavery and prior to colonization of the African continent, the Pope along with other Europeans may have seen the Africans as super humans, in terms of their physical ability to do hard work in a harsh environment. Once they realized that Africans were no different than other human beings, the movement to end slavery began in earnest spearheaded by the churches.

We cannot talk about the slave trade along the West Coast of Africa, where the Europeans were the main traders, without mentioning the parallel slave trade along the East Coast of Africa and the Sub-Sahara, where the Arabs were the sole traders. In fact, what saved West Africans from the crueler Arab slave traders was the rainforest, which bred the tsetse fly, an insect that was a deadly enemy to their horses.

The discussion of Arab slave trade is important because in their frustration, brought about by perceived inability to compete with their fellow Americans who happen to be whites, some black Americans have turned to Islam because they perceive it as a religion of non-oppressors. The perception of the messengers of Islam, who are mainly Arabs, as non-oppressors is erroneous. Three factors may have contributed to this erroneous perception. First, we will use sports analogy to understand the mentality at play in this subject. When two teams play against each other, even though one loses the match, the losing team does not see this loss as the end of the world; instead, it believes that it may come back and win in the next game. That means that the losing team does not see the winning team as being so superior that it can never be defeated. In this case members of the losing team may feel sad for losing but a strong emotion of defeatism or helplessness is not involved. The translation is that, psychologically, those Blacks who tend to turn to Islam may feel a lot more at ease sitting next to a Muslim than a white person, in most circumstances, because they do not perceive the Muslims as culturally or intellectually superior.

Secondly, black Americans who read history of the slave trade may have only concentrated on the part that involved the Europeans. It reinforces the narrative, by some Blacks, that Whites are evil because they did a terrible thing to black people and, therefore, must pay for it. Blacks who only think along this line are blinded from true history by nature generated frustration. That frustration has prevented them from accepting the fact that white people were not solely responsible for the slave trade. There were enough blames to go around in that dark phase of human development. Besides, it is more profitable to accuse white people of historical injustices, especially with the prevailing atmosphere of political correctness and minority appeasement. They forget that the hardest thing to change in a people is their cultural behavior. Clan and tribal wars had existed in the African continent before the Europeans first set foot there. It was the wars that initiated slavery in the continent. Even after European colonization, tribalism and clannishness are still very much alive in Africa. Some people in Africa today still carry tribal marks meant to identify what tribe or clan they come from, which is a leftover from the clan and tribal war era. Twenty-first century politics in the African continent is highly influenced by tribal loyalty.

Thirdly, some black Americans may be drawn to Islam by the same motivation as they are drawn to the Democratic Party of today, which may be related to material benefits from the relationship. They disregard the fact that it was the Europeans, with England leading the way, that eventually decided to stop the slave trade, not the Africans and not the Arabs. Also, the favorite political party of black Americans, the Democratic Party, was the same party whose ancestor fought tooth and nail to keep the ancestors of black Americans in slavery indefinitely. In fact, left for the Arabs, the slave trade would have raged on till this day. Today, the descendents of those Arab slave traders are sitting on huge oil wealth and are in a position to buy followership for their religion and friendship for themselves with generous donations.

I think that the lesson we can all learn about slavery was that it happened at the time we knew little or nothing about each other; we were all objects of curiosity to one another. After all, to assume that the Europeans knew exactly what they were doing or were capable of looking far into the future to see exactly how it was all going to turn out is naïve at the best. Nor does anyone doubt that had the role been reversed, where the Africans had been more advanced, they would not have taken the Europeans across the ocean to work in plantations in their new colonies. If anyone is in doubt, just observe what happens in the United States now. When black Americans are put in a position of power, which may be as simple as being a juror in a criminal trial, there have been instances where they had decided to free a black person accused of killing a white person, but had voted to convict a white person accused under a similar charge. They believe this behavior to be justified because white jurors used to do the same thing when black people had no power. So, you wonder when the seesaw behavior is going to end, and who is going to be civilized enough to discard the bad experience and show the other a better way to live.

5. FORMER EUROPEAN COLONIES IN THE AMERICAS AND THEIR INHERITANCE

A fellow from South America once told me at a party that he believed that Great Britain did not apply the same policies in its colonies in India and the black African countries as in the United States, Australia, Canada, and South Africa. That was supposed to be an explanation for the reason why these four countries were able to rise from being colonies to being developed modern societies, while other former British colonies still remain underdeveloped. For the French, Spanish, and Portuguese former colonies, the argument is that the colonizers did not intend to develop their former colonies but to exploit their resources for the betterment of the colonizers. That also means that there was no attempt to give the natives education and teach them how to build their countries into modern societies, if and when they become independent.

The fact is that if we look around, we can find countries that were never colonized by Europeans but still become developed modern societies. Good examples of such non-European countries that were never colonized by Europeans are Japan and South Korea. Except for a brief occupation by Italy during World War II, Ethiopia was never colonized but there is no sign that it is becoming a developed modern society anytime soon. Liberia and Haiti have been independent countries for over 150 years now, enough time to enable the people to figure out how to move their countries forward, but they both seem to be mired in cycle of poverty and corruption as well as political and social crisis.

These arguments camouflage the real reason why some countries are hindered from developing. The real reason is cultural. The former English colonies that become developed were controlled and run by settlers of European descent; the culture they brought with them to the colonies was the same as that of England. While every culture has good and bad aspects, the European culture has produced overwhelmingly more positive results than other cultures, to which majority of the underdeveloped countries belong. Culture is the key to putting the Europeans ahead of the other races. The European culture creates an environment that allows the individual to exercise his mind with little restrictions. This explains why a lot of capable people from underdeveloped countries blossom once they immigrate to developed countries.

The Spanish speaking countries of the Americas, which send the largest number of immigrants into the United States, have not presented a good explanation of why the countries are unable to develop their societies to even one-third the level of development reached by the United States and Canada. Apparently everyone that has been involved in the argument over legal and illegal immigration has unscrupulously shied away from discussing and addressing the roots of the disparities between the United States and Canada on one side and the Spanish speaking countries of the Americas on the other side. Mexico represents the ultimate phenomenon of the stark disparity because it has existed side-by-side with the United States for centuries, and yet the difference between the two countries is like day and night. Someone who has never been to North America before can travel from Canada through the United States without noticing a difference between the two countries until he crosses into Mexico. There seem to be no hope that the situation in Mexico is moving towards improvement that would enable the people to have the same standard of living as their northern neighbors. Instead, it is most likely that the entire population of Mexico may literally empty itself into its northern neighbors if allowed to do so.

The unfortunate thing about the situation in Spanish speaking America is that the blame is not being placed squarely where it truly belongs. Instead, Americans are blamed if they oppose mass immigration as desired by Hispanics to give them more political clout. Nobody queries why politicians who run those countries are unable to manage their natural resources with honesty and greater efficiency for the benefit of the people. Hispanics in the United States should have been working together with the government of the United States to pressure Latin American governments to reform their cultural behaviors and abandon corruption so that those countries can move forward.

Instead, they find it easier to pressure the United States because it is a more responsive society than the ones in Latin America. Fortunately for them, one side of the American political spectrum has decided to harness the illegal immigration issue to garner Hispanic votes, even though large scale unchecked immigration is bound to have adverse effect on this society somewhere down the road, and when that happens, everyone in this country will pay the price.

The United States has become a country that is now so divided that it is quickly eating itself up literally, with one political party now willing to give the country away for votes or to whoever complains or threatens. The question we should all honestly ask ourselves is: if the Hispanics are unable to develop their countries of origin, would they be able to run the United States relatively well, as was the case when they immigrated here seeking a better life, or would they default to the way the Spanish speaking countries are currently run? There is an expression that you can take a man out of a culture but only he can take the culture out of himself. There is nothing in their behaviors regarding language, culture, and voting pattern that shows that they intend to keep America the way it was when they immigrated. Until there is a single developed and well managed Spanish speaking country in the Americas, there is no hope that the United States would survive when it falls under the control of Hispanics. Based on their voting records so far, Hispanics seem to vote only on a one-track issue of immigration, regardless of what is happening to the society economically and socially. Besides, Hispanics have demonstrated that they follow a tribal voting pattern when a Hispanic candidate contests an election against a non-Hispanic candidate. They overwhelmingly vote for the Hispanic candidate except when the candidate sees things differently on immigration.

Hispanics vote overwhelmingly for the Democratic Party because they believe that the party tacitly embraces wide open door immigration, legal and illegal, while they see the Republican Party as wanting to control the flow of illegal immigration by tightening the border and enforcing the law against companies that employ illegal immigrants. However, this perception of the Republican Party by Hispanics is not only unfair but also appears to show ingratitude. In 1986 the very first mass amnesty for illegal immigrants, which boosted the Hispanics population and voters tremendously, was signed by President Ronald Reagan, a Republican. The amnesty was granted based on a deal reached with Congress to tighten the border and embark on vigorous internal enforcement against employers of illegal immigrants. The amnesty was granted as agreed but the border control and internal enforcement were neglected or abandoned. Today, the estimate is that illegal immigrant population has topped 12 million, a number that rivals the population of many countries around the world. In spite of the fact that a Republican president presided over the very first amnesty, the party was never rewarded with overwhelming Hispanics votes since 1986. Why the ingratitude on the part of the Hispanics? It appears that nothing short of handing the United States over to them to run will satisfy the Hispanics.

The fact is that Hispanics do not want to see the border controlled or closed to illegal immigration nor see internal enforcement implemented because they still want their relatives and friends, who they cannot bring into the United State legally, enter the country illegally just like those before them, and the Democratic Party seems to be just happy to oblige them. So, for the Republican Party, the relationship with Hispanics voters has become one of damn if you do and damn if you don't. If the Republican Party tries to compete with the Democratic Party's politics of votes-for-favors, the downfall of the United States of America will accelerate exponentially. If the Republican Party really believes that it is the party of principle, as it claims, then it should stand up for what is good for this country. When falsely accused of racism, it should respond by saying that if policies designed to keep America a viable country economically, socially, and militarily is labeled racist by those who by commission or omission want to destroy the country, then saving the country for everybody that lives in it is a more noble cause. At some point, the Republican Party may decide that it is better to go down fighting than to embark on appeasement that just makes things worse. Hopefully, history will show that it fought very hard to save America from both internal and external forces of decline. White America has to realize, too, that not being racist does not mean that it has to stand by or go along with policies and leadership of anyone or party that will lead to the decline or destruction of this country regardless of the ethnicity of the president.

Hispanic voters also do owe it to themselves and their offspring to keep America better than the countries they left behind because if this society gets overwhelmed and falls into serious political, economic, and social crisis, it won't be worth a place to live in or feel safe. Without strong economic growth, there will be no immigration and those that are already here may have no choice but to leave, if they still have families elsewhere. Those who can't leave may stay and face whatever comes. As the Democratic Party keeps overloading the population of the United States with new immigrants and dumping them into the welfare system, so that it can stay in power forever, it is doubtful that a one-party system is going to be acceptable to many Americans because that defaults to dictatorship. There is always a breaking point in any human situation, and sometimes, it may turn out to be better to have a smaller and more peaceful society than to have a huge crisis-laden society. As evolutionists can agree, even the universe blew up because staying together created too much friction.

Without economic power, the United States may no longer be a military power, and may be picked on by even smaller but more aggressive countries or organized groups. As if to add insult to injury, as a divided country, the United States may face internal sabotage and will not effectively defend itself. The country's stockpile of weapons of mass destruction will be useless under a situation where internal disunity is coupled with attacks from outside aggressors. This scenario may sound farfetched to some people but judging from our current political atmosphere, where one side appears to be willing to give the country away for the immediate gain of votes and power, which allows it to force its social and political agenda on society, there is a possibility that things might reach a boiling point as we continue to drift farther apart ideologically. It is irrational to expect the best result, if such corrupt political strategy pursued by the Democratic Party persists. The other side may decide to adopt other tactics that might have seemed inconceivable previously. After all, we have to remember that this country was designed to be a republic and not a democracy, specifically to avoid the use of all forms of Machiavellianism, including bribery, to win elections and then subjugate a minority to unacceptable political and social ideologies.

6. WILL SOCIALISM WORK IN AMERICA?

As a high school student in Nigeria in the early 60's, I thought that the newly independent African nations should adapt the socialist system of government. That desire for socialist type of government in the newly independent African countries was influenced by several concerns of mine. The first was that tribal politics was too strong and was not going to allow Africans to elect capable and honest leaders. The assumption was that the socialist leaders who were going to run the countries would be a special caliber of leaders who would be competent and above corruption, mismanagement, and nepotism. My second concern was corruption, which I believed would not allow honest democratic elections to take root in the continent. Thirdly, I thought that a socialist government would usher in a new era in educational opportunities and true development for all the countries. I have since realized that progress and development are really driven by the quality of the people and their culture. Progress will not take place in a corrupt culture regardless of the system of government.

The situation gets even worst in a socialist system because it kills the individual's creative nature. If people are free to create, a few exceptional individuals, at least, can revolutionize society and open a new horizon for everyone. After all, out of the billions of people on earth, only exceptionally intelligent and talented few have given us the knowledge that had enabled mankind to advance to where we are today. I think of human progress in terms of a pyramid, where few highly talented people and inventors at the top set off a chain reaction that spreads down to the base of the pyramid. When a gifted person comes up with a new invention or new idea, others below him on the pyramid break down the invention or idea. Once the invention is translated into practical use, even those that can neither invent nor build learn how to use the products and ideas to improve their lives.

Socialism would never be able to make everybody a doctor, scientist, engineer, accountant, and successful entrepreneur, even if it makes education free for everybody from elementary school to university. I used to think that it was only a lack of opportunity that prevented people from going to college, but those were my days of naiveté's about life. Some people are simply not cut out to go to college, but may be endowed with other talents or develop other skills that enable them to make a better living than college graduates. Others that are not endowed with any useful talent and are unable to learn any talent contend themselves with what nature gives them. There are people who are naturally unable to set a goal and pursue it to a logical conclusion. Either way, we have to understand that these people cannot explain why they are unable to do something worthwhile with their lives because it was nature that set them up to be that way. The question is, does the whole society have an obligation to take responsibility for its members that nature gave no ability to achieve a better life than where they find themselves, or should their family and charity work together to help these people get through life? Should socialism decide that if a third of a society is not productive enough, for reasons that have nothing to do with physical or mental disability, the other two-thirds of society must be forced to provide them the same standard of living as everyone else?

I grew up in a farming community where people were expected to get up early in the morning and start working in the field. They took a break when the sun got too hot and went back to the field when the Sun became less intense and worked until sunset. Those were the ones that earned more money after the yearly harvest. But there were some other farmers that were not as hard working and spent most of the time in other less productive activities. Sometimes, they work in the morning and nap all afternoon and never went back to the field for the rest of the day. People admire the hardworking individuals and preferred to marry them. The lazy and less hard working ones were not very respected in the community. Other farmers always volunteered to help harvest the crops of any farmer whose fields were under threat of being flooded during heavy rainfall. If someone went hunting and was successful, he would make sure that his neighbors get pieces from the kill. The same goes for a farmer that made an extraordinary catch in a fishing trip. It will be quite unnatural for the government to tell the hardworking farmer that it would take proceeds from his yearly harvest and distribute it to the other farmers that did not work as hard.

The socialist revolutions and military coups that swept through the newly independent countries of Africa, Latin America, and Asia in the

60's and 70's produced no positive changes for the people. The ills of corruption, mismanagement, and plain incompetence continued in the ex-European colonies of Africa and Latin America. Successive revolutions, usually by the military, to reform the previous one that had become corrupt simply resulted in more corruption. With time, the old politicians that negotiated with the colonialists for independence and who, in fact, turned out to be less corrupt, were gone and those running the so-called third world countries now are young, mostly college-educated but, unfortunately, more corrupt than the generation of politicians before them. If anything, they have gotten more sophisticated in the art of corruption.

America spent enormous resources staving off socialism from newly independent developing countries for decades at the time USSR and China were actively pushing the socialist-communist ideology on the vulnerable young countries. But now, it appears that America herself is blindly moving towards the failed socialist ideology, as if the country is suffering from a serious case of political amnesia. How can that be? I doubt that American people fully consent to be taken in that direction; instead, it is clear that they were lured onto that path. Radical progressives are using socialist principles under the guise of social justice to destroy America. If Barack Obama isn't the reincarnation of Pied Piper of Hamelin now leading American Blacks, youths, Hispanics, Asians, and immigrants off the cliff I don't know who is.

7. SOCIALISM AS A COLD WAR TOOL

The socialist revolutions of the 60's and 70's were tools used by the USSR and China to prosecute the Cold War. Their strategy was to use the newly independent countries of Africa and the underdeveloped countries of Asia and Latin America as proxies. Some of the revolutionaries had studied in some East Bloc countries before returning to their home countries. They usually go into the jungle or the mountain to set up training camps. They would then recruit young people from the countryside and poor neighborhoods because those were the ones most likely to be resentful of the rich and middle class in the country. Once they have received enough clandestine arms and funds from the communist bloc countries the revolutionaries then start off by blowing up roads, bridges, and buildings. Other road to socialist revolution most common in the underdeveloped countries of Asia, African, and Latin America was military coup by usually young military officers who upon taking control of the government promptly declared the country a socialist republic. However, it was one thing to overthrow a duly elected government through guerrilla warfare or military coup but another thing to rid society of the cultural behavior that breed corruption, and then run the country efficiently.

The socialist revolutions failed because the leaders realized that they were literally fighting against the nature of human beings. Human beings are part of nature that we can communicate with but still not be able to mold into what we want. When you make rules that force people to do something against their nature, especially under the threat of punishment or death, they will go along with your rules but they will eventually become despondent, less creative, and less productive. Their lack of creativity will be a loss to society. They will only do the minimum required of them to stay out of trouble. That was the situation in the USSR and China during their attempts to create a communist society. Now Russia is a democratic country while China is gradually allowing its citizens to embark on private enterprise. Life in both countries has seen political and economic improvements.

The United States committed resources and efforts to prevent the spread of communism to the emerging nations. The countries of Africa just emerging from colonial rule were most vulnerable to the idea that socialism would bring rapid development and equal opportunity for all citizens. Although colonization did not infringe upon personal liberty in these countries, there a false perception that their national resources were being exploited for the benefits of the colonizers. It took independence or self rule for the people to realize how wrong that perception was. The native politicians quickly took corruption to a level never imagined before. Inefficiency and mismanagement became the order of the day. These ills caused the people to believe that socialism could restrict those behaviors, but what they did not consider is that their culture was the source of the problem. A few countries that actually tried to establish socialist government failed woefully because they could not get rid of corruption at the highest level of government. Eventually, the idea of socialism was completely dropped everywhere after the USSR disbanded and abandoned communism.

The Cold War ended for the developing countries with really nothing to show for it, except that they did not end up with governments telling the people how to live their lives. The United States succeeded in containing communism but not the flow of immigrants from the countries it saved from communism; in other words, giving the threatened people their freedom didn't mean that they were going to stay home and develop their countries. So, regardless of the kind of government or economic system a country ends up with, the people are still going to be seeking a better life elsewhere as long as they are unable to rid themselves of corruption, mismanagement, and inefficiency that are rooted in their cultural behaviors.

8. AMERICA AND THE COLD WAR

The 1960's were the era of independence from colonial rules for many black African countries. While independence came through constitutional conference for the English colonies some French and

Portuguese colonies fought against the colonial rulers to win their independence. Regardless of which European countries colonized the African countries, there was a great deal of expectations by the colonized Africans that independence would bring rapid development, since one of the promises of independence from colonial rule was that the natural resources of the colonies would be for the natives and not harvested and carted away for the enrichment of the colonizers. Independence would put the natives in charge of their natural resources and political destiny.

Soon after World War II (WWII), the United States and the former Soviet Union (USSR) began to have a falling out, driven by political ideologies; the Chinese soon joined the capitalism versus communism post-WWII Cold War. The objective of the USSR and China was to spread communism all over the world while the United States' objective was to contain the spread of communism. Actually, the Cold War wasn't so cold for the countries they were trying to influence one way or the other. The newly independent African countries as well as the underdeveloped countries of Asia and Latin America were the actual battle grounds where people physically died as a result of the revolutions and military coup d'état, some of which ended up in outright civil wars.

While USSR and China provided arms and clandestine training for guerrilla warfare to socialist or communist revolutionaries in the countries they targeted, the United States provided arms and training to support duly elected or existing governments. Some of the countries supported by the United States were understandably headed by monarchs. The United States also provided support to anti-communist military officers to overthrow elected governments that were turning their countries into socialist states. USSR and China were careful not to be involved physically in the revolutions, but used proxies to attack United States' interests and prosecute the Cold War. Although the United States wasn't as covert as the USSR and China, it never sent combat troops to participate in the overthrow of elected governments in the emerging African countries and Latin America, but that was not the case in Vietnam and Korea. Its involvement in Korea was under the guise of United Nations resolution but started out the Vietnam War involvement through the usual military coup tactic. Then one thing led to another and the United States became involved in a full scale war against North Vietnamese communists and South Vietnamese communists nicknamed "Vietcong." Perhaps, if the United States had not intervened in Vietnam and allowed the communist flame to burn out by itself, just like in the USSR and China, over 58,000 Americans would not have died, and the dramatic flow of Vietnamese refugees to the US would not have been the case.

The United States use of military advisers in some Latin American countries was well known. A few well-liked African leaders like

Kwame Nkrumah of Ghana and Patrice Lumumba of the Congo were victims of CIA covert activities during the Cold War. Almost every Latin American country was affected in different degrees by the 60's socialist revolutions during the Cold War. Cuba survived invasion by exiles trained and armed by the United States. Regardless of the outcome of the attempt by socialist revolutionaries to overthrow duly elected governments anywhere in the developing nations, socialism failed as a viable economic system in those countries. The socialist system they tried to establish did not work because it goes contrary to the nature of the people. Subsequently the USSR broke up and every country that emerged from the former Soviet Union abandoned communism. China is the only country that is still hanging on to some remnants of the communist system that Mao established after his 1949 revolution. It is possible that the Chinese government is fearful that without some control, its huge population could fall into chaos, reminiscent of the pre-revolution era.

In the final analysis, even though the United States emerged victorious from the Cold War it did not walk out of it without some bruises of its own. Thousands of American soldiers died in South Vietnam and Korea. South Vietnam was quickly overrun by communist North Vietnam as soon as the United States pulled out. Korea may seem like a success story if you consider the progress that South Korea has made under continued United States protection, but the danger isn't over yet in the Korean Peninsula as long as the two Koreas are not united. Secondly, because of more aggressive covert participation by the United States and the presence of advisers as opposed to the use of proxies by USSR and China to prosecute their Cold War strategy, there was a perception that the United States was the initiator of the Cold War. Of course, if those who think so were to be a little more honest, they would ask themselves if the USSR and China really had institutional or physical investments that needed to be protected in the countries in which they were pushing communist or socialist revolutions on. You can imagine those two countries as having nothing to lose by having proxies blow up buildings, bridges, roads, and factories in developing countries. They did not own any of those structures being blown up. United States and Western Europe had a lot of investments in the underdeveloped countries. However, for emerging as the winner of the Cold War, domestic radical progressives, socialists, communists, trade unionists, and their foreign allies viewed the United States as the sole superpower that meddled in the affairs of perceived powerless countries.

As memories of the Cold War began to fade, even Western Europeans that hid behind the United States during the Cold War began to mumble some complaint because they now want to be consulted whenever the United States decides that it has some interest to defend or protect somewhere. In reality, the European complaint is driven by camouflaged human envy of those that are perceived to be so powerful that they can't be defeated no matter how much you try. That kind of thinking makes one feel smaller, psychologically, to the perceived undefeatable person, and causes the envious to wish that the powerful bumps its toe on some rock and fall. You can remember that the United States has been attacked over many years by terrorists, but rarely did any country introduce a resolution in the UN condemning the acts of terrorism, not even after 9-11, a terrorist attack that I was convinced that many Europeans silently applauded. The Europeans may offer some benign reasons for the formation of the European Union but I am convinced that it was formed to counter the United States economic and military influence; after all, they no longer face any threat from communism as was the case during the Cold War. Now, it is safe to crawl out of the rock under which they have been hiding to undermine the erstwhile protector, but who they now view as a dominator.

Barrack Obama may have been a teenager when the Cold War ended but he had studied the era from the point of view of his radical college professors. The problem with radicals is that they lack balance and, therefore, incapable of looking at any issue from all angles. You can recall that when he addressed the Arabs in Cairo during his United States-condemnation world tour, he told his listeners that they had been used as pawns during the Cold War. Blinded by his eagerness to condemn the country that has just elected him its president, Barack Obama forgot that natural contradictions exist between Islam, or any other religion for that matter, and communism. So, those Muslim countries needed no American to tell them which side they wanted to win the Cold War. That should have been obvious to the Harvard educated president. In fact, some of his listeners at the Cairo speech may have been the Jihadists that fought the Soviet Military in Afghanistan. They fought against the Soviets during the Cold War because communism was intruding on their traditional hierarchical culture and religion. During the condemnation tours in Europe and the Middle East, Obama portrayed the United States as an arrogant country that was at times dismissive and even derisive. Finally, the Europeans have found an American that voiced what they have been thinking ever since the end of the Cold War. Therefore, for the condemnation of the United States, Barack Obama was rewarded with the Nobel Prize.

The Cold War was not only fought with covert activities such as military training and arms supplies, it also involved some other peaceful activities on both sides, if only with some ulterior motives. As part of their Cold War strategy, the USSR and China were offering scholarships through local trade unions to young Africans to study in their universities. As you can imagine, those countries where the governments were not leaning towards socialism, the East Bloc scholarships were not overtly offered, instead, the trade union leaders picked their relatives and those of their friends first; the leftovers were sold to others who simply wanted opportunity to study abroad regardless of where they had to go. Those who received the scholarships usually travelled to the East Bloc countries covertly. The fact that the scholarships were given on the basis of nepotism and bribery more than explains how the socialist trade unionists would have run their respective countries, if they had power.

In the early 70's I had met some African students who went to study in the USSR under those trade union scholarships here in the United States. I guess that in an attempt to show that the USSR did not restrict the movement of the foreign students, the scholarship program allowed the students to go anywhere they wanted during the summer break. Those who chose to spend their summer in the United States, perhaps, because they knew someone here, never went back to the USSR. They were full of stories of scarcities of simple things that they took for granted, even in their own home countries, and lack of recreation. Of course, their idea of recreation probably meant disco night clubs. Also, unlike in the United States the USSR and China did not have a host family program where a foreign student is adopted by an American family and spend time with them during breaks from their studies. Those that received scholarships to study in China complained about many restrictions imposed on them by the Chinese authorities. They were not allowed to have parties or date Chinese girls. Well aware of the sacrifice that its poor citizens were making to provide scholarships to students from other poor countries, I guess that the Chinese government expected the scholarship beneficiaries to concentrate only on their studies with no distraction whatsoever. Even though there might have been some racial component to the restrictions the Chinese authority placed on African students, I did sympathize with the side of the Chinese authority. Those African students should have been aware of what they were walking into when they applied for those trade union scholarships with communist China as the benefactor.

The United States' peaceful Cold War strategy was two pronged. One aspect involved direct scholarships to African countries through their governments. Some students also obtained scholarships directly from some American institutions funded by some private organizations. Some African governments also awarded scholarships to their young students to study in Western universities, especially the United States and Britain. Some of the scholarships were also made available by funds from private organizations. One of the East African students who benefitted from scholarships provided by a private organization was Barack Hussein Obama (Sr.), the supposed father of Barack Hussein Obama (II), the President of the United States. He came in 1959 during what was nicknamed "The Airlift" which Obama mentioned in one of his speeches, except that he falsely claimed that it was ordered by President John F. Kennedy (JFK). The second strategy used by the United States was the Peace Corp Volunteer Program, which was instituted by JFK. The Peace Corp Program sent young American college students, graduates, and others with some skill as volunteers to teach in high schools and trade schools in various developing countries. The volunteers also worked in selected villages, teaching the farmers new farming skills and how to build irrigation systems and wells to obtain water from the ground. The Peace Corp program was probably the most enduring program that came out of the Cold War era. It was highly valuable and appreciated by the host countries. I had several Peace Corp volunteers in my high school and we enjoyed having the young Americans because they were easy going and friendly and quite refreshing from the rigid business-like British that we were used to.

The success of the Peace Corp Program was, however, contradicted by events in Southeast Asia, where the same JFK kicked up the dust that got the ball rolling in the Vietnam conflict. He also presided over the invasion of Cuba that brought the world to the brink of a nuclear war. Perhaps, if he had handled the Cuban revolution properly, Cubans would have abandoned communism sooner and returned to the natural way of living, which is freedom of the individual and the free enterprise system. Even though Obama in one of his resentful statements claimed that the free market system has never worked and will never work, it did work for the United States, which is why he is here instead of being in China, Indonesia, or Kenya. The peace and war legacies of the venerable JFK go to show that you cannot assign the title of war monger solely to the Republicans or the Democrats. Any American president, regardless of party affiliation, would fight if he or she believes that America or its interest is threatened anywhere in the world. However, that is now changing because the United States seems to be in the process of being delivered to the control of the United Nations, for keeps, under Barack Obama and the new generation of the Democratic Party.

9. OBAMA'S CONNECTION TO THE COLD WAR

The story Obama told America about his biological origin was that his father grew up in Kenya, in East Africa, herding goats. In an address to a largely black audience during a commemoration of the 1965 Selma Alabama march, he added another dimension to the story. He told the audience that his father "won one of several tickets" (scholarships) offered by JFK when he ordered that young Africans be brought to the United States under a program nicknamed "Air Lift" to see what a wonderful country America is. In the same speech, he told a brief story about how his father and mother met. According to him, they met during the Selma Alabama march and decided that the atmosphere was right to get together and have a child, and Barack Jr. was born. Obama was applauded at each punch line in his speech by the audience.

If ever there was a false prophet, Obama was and is still a very successful one. A documentary produced by Joel Gilbert titled "Dreams from My Real Father" (Highway 61 Entertainment), has added a huge question mark in Barack Obama's biological story. The fact is that the two statements he made during the commemoration of the 1965 Selma Alabama march were and are still inaccurate. First, let's examine how and why his supposed Kenyan father came to study in the United States in 1959. This was the period that the Cold War was adding new strategy to the arms race. The new strategy had to do with winning the hearts and minds of people in the hitherto European colonies of Africa about to become independent and join the ranks of the UN general assembly as voting members. The United States wouldn't want to have all those black African countries always voting with the opposite side, would it? There was another element to the East African Air Lift program. The "Mau Mau" rebellion against the British colonialists by the natives was put down by the colonial authority in 1959. The Mau Mau was a secret cult organized by the natives to terrorize the white people, mostly the British in Kenya. Their tactic was to attack families in isolated areas. They would kill everyone in a family, including house bets, and decapitate their bodies. It was organized by mostly members of the majority Kikuyu tribe of Kenya. Obama's supposed father belonged to the rival Luo tribe.

Unfortunately, this kind of barbarism gets a lot of attention and curiosity, and it wouldn't be farfetched to imagine that some anti-colonialists in the United States could have viewed the rebellion as a legitimate act of defiance against colonial rule. The result was that even before JFK came to power, some individuals and organizations have already started to raise funds to bring Kenyan students to study in the United States, so that they could be better prepared to help the new independent Kenya when the time comes. Among some of the contributors to the Air Lift fund were some black American activists. I think that it is worthwhile to mention that the grant of independence to Kenya was not hastened by the Mau Mau rebellion. After all, grant of independence to British African colonies did not involve any bloodshed but was based on the lesson England learned after the loss of the American colony. Following the loss of the American colony, Great Britain wisely realized that it was not going to hold any colony forever. Therefore, a new colonial policy was formulated, which established that the goal of Great Britain would be to prepare people of any new colony for independence by giving them good education to help them establish a democratic system of government.

Britain made education a priority in every country it colonized after the American colony. That accounts for the reason why there were more educated natives in former British African colonies than in countries colonized by other Europeans. The new colonial policy created a smooth transition from colonial rule to independence without bloodshed. The process of granting independence involved constitutional conference with representatives of the colonizer and the colonized setting the timetable for independence. That was followed by a general election in the colony, and the handover of the administration of the country to the new government elected by the natives. The peaceful transfer of rule to the natives fostered a free membership and participation in the British Commonwealth of Nations.

Notice that Obama's supposed Kenyan father arrived in Hawaii in 1959 prior to JFK being inaugurated as the President of the United States in 1960. If anybody should be able to distinguish the timeline between those two events, I expected a Harvard educated constitutional lawyer to be on top of the list. JFK had nothing to do with Barack Obama (Sr.'s) journey to Hawaii to study in the University of Hawaii in 1959 but the Air Lift was part of the United States' Cold War strategy. Ironically, the first post-independence prime minister of Kenya, Jomo Kenyatta, a member of the Kikuyu tribe and commonly referred to as the father of Kenya's independence, was a pro-Western and anti-communist politician. His imprisonment during the Mau Mau rebellion did not make a socialist out of him. On the other hand, upon finally returning to Kenya, after studying in Harvard, Obama's supposed father began to promote the socialist system of government for his country. Obviously, he was willing to benefit from American education but not the political and economic systems that gave birth to the excellent educational system.

Obama's second inaccurate statement at the Selma Alabama commemoration speech was that his parents met during the march and decided that the time was ripe to get together and have Barack Jr. Again, here is why that is disappointedly inaccurate for a Harvard educated constitutional lawyer: Barack Hussein Obama II was born in 1961 in Hawaii, and the Selma Alabama march took place in 1965, which was four long years after he was born. Barack Hussein Obama would have been born a second time or you may call him a "born again child" for his parents to have met at that event and decided to have him. Ironically, it all seems to fit into the man's character, when you come to think about it. He seems to constantly reinvent himself in order to fit in or get ahead wherever he is.

Any which way you look at the foundation of Obama's life you would have no other choice but to conclude that he is a product of the Cold War, not a Cold War warrior but an offspring with the Cold War busting out from his veins. In his documentary, Dreams from My Real Father, Joel Gilbert presented powerful evidence that the avowed black American communist, Frank Marshall Davis, was indeed the biological father of Barack Obama. According to the documentary, Obama's grandfather, Stanley Dunham, was a CIA operative who was stationed in Hawaii to keep an eye on American communists during the Cold War. Frank Marshall Davis was the main target of his assignment. When the East African Air Lift was initiated, he was also assigned to take care of the students coming in on the air lift. He befriended both Frank Marshall Davis and the Kenyan student, Barack Hussein Obama (Sr.) who came in with the air lift. The documentary showed how one thing led to another and his daughter, Ann Stanley Dunham, became pregnant with Frank Marshall Davis' child, now known as Barack Hussein Obama II, the President of the United States of America.

It would have been extremely awkward for Obama's grandfather if it had become known that his daughter became pregnant by an avowed communist that he was assigned to watch. So, he convinced the Kenyan student he was handling to accept responsibility for the pregnancy. The documentary speculated that Obama (Jr.) may have found out somewhere along the way that Frank Marshall Davis was his real father. Although Obama's autobiography, Dreams from My Father, is full of references to "Uncle Frank" as his mentor while growing up, Obama's psychological makeup had already decided that a more exotic father would be one that came from a far away country that many Americans know very little about. That accounts for the alternating story of going back to Indonesia or Kenya to become a ruler that he peddled in his school in Hawaii.

Unfortunately, all the people that could have revealed the truth about Obama's biological father, such as his mother, grandfather, Barack Obama (Sr.) of Kenya, and Frank Marshall Davis are no longer alive. One possibility of obtaining the proof is to exhume the remains of Frank Marshall Davis and compare his DNA with that of Barack Obama (II). Of course, that proposal amounts to wishful thinking because

Barack Obama is already on top of the world, and couldn't care less what anybody thinks or believes. He has pulled the biggest con in the history of mankind and nobody can take the loot away from him now. I suspect that when Obama's grandfather got older and retired from the CIA, it didn't matter to him anymore what Frank Marshall Davis taught his grandson.

10. CULTURAL CHANGES AND THEIR DECAYING EFFECTS

A few years after I have been living in the United States, I began to feel concerned about the cultural changes in the society that I observed evolving. I noticed that immigrants tend to cluster in a section of the city they live mostly along the line of national origin. This allows them to recreate the society that they left behind literally. Why anybody would want to take along with him something that had failed to work for him wherever he goes may make a research subject for a whole new book. Many, especially the ones that came from Spanish speaking America through the US-Mexican border appear to make no efforts to learn English because they are able to survive living around other Spanish speaking immigrants and working at jobs where the supervisor speaks Spanish. They usually find work through relatives and friends from the same country of origin. As uncontrolled and unmanaged immigration, especially from the southern border of the country continues, this situation is expected to worsen. It appears that immigrants come to the United States with the sole goal of finding jobs. They know that they can find jobs easier and make more money than they could in their own country. But they seem less conscientious about what else makes the United States different from their country of birth, and they are very likely to try to carry on with their cultural behaviors. Remember that the culture they are trying to recreate in the United States is the very same culture that had kept their country of origin underdeveloped.

While very few voices have warned about this, majority of Americans simply shrug their shoulders and seemed unconcerned about this issue. Instead, immigration appeared to be viewed as a source of cheap labor and large number of undisciplined consumers. American corporations and businesses appeared to depend on constant population growth, through immigration, to compensate for their competitive disadvantage in world market for their manufactured products. With cheap labor and consumers pouring into the country literally on a daily basis, they need not worry about competing in the global market.

When the Democratic Party realized that immigrants-turned-citizens could provide it with votes to stay in power, legal and illegal immigration exploded in the United States. The Republican Party was also complicit to some extent because it accepted the situation in order to please businesses that benefit from it. Today, we have reached the point of no return, and the country can either continue on its steady march towards becoming a country midway between a first and third world society, socially and economically, or face a civil war that could most likely break up the country. As I observe American-born citizens shrug their shoulders about the cultural effect of uncontrolled immigration, I began to realize that I am witnessing the same events and behaviors reminiscent of the decline and fall of the Roman Empire, as I read in my high school ancient history. The decline of an empire or a civilization has a way of camouflaging itself. At the height of the success of the Roman Empire, complacency took over. Great Roman generals and noblemen began to indulge themselves in immoral life styles. They did not see the life style as immoral behaviors; instead, the behaviors were accepted as the next rung in their civilization ladder. Those who did not participate in the immoral activities were considered backward, out of touch, and unimportant, much the same as the situation in the United States today where progressives think that the sky should be the limit of what society can accept as norm. But the immoral behaviors caused the Roman Empire to become weak and unable to defend itself when barbarians and less civilized enemies came knocking on the empire's gates. The Romans even thought that they could train thousands of guest workers as soldiers and place them under the command of Roman generals, but it did not work out very well. The guest workers did not fight with the same spirit as the Roman soldiers or were just not skilled enough.

Immigration has been part of human experience since the beginning of time. Before man's civilization began to create villages, towns, and cities, I imagine that people would move from areas of less fertile land, less water, and less productive hunting ground to other places with more abundant supplies. Once they get there, they would either have to negotiate with those who were already occupying the area for a piece of land to settle or they may resort to force to get themselves into the land. As civilization began to advance and human beings began to build villages, towns, and cities, immigration dramatically increased. All the past civilizations received immigrants from less civilized places but immigration always played a role in the decline of past civilizations. The reason for this may be explained by the principle of osmosis. Human immigration obeys the principle of osmosis, which says that if two unequally concentrated solutions are placed side-by-side and separated by a thin membrane, the solution with a weaker concentration would sip into the solution with a higher concentration until the two solutions become equal in concentration. The bigger the difference in concentration between the solutions the higher the sipping rate from the less concentrated solution to the solution with higher concentration. That may explain the apparent rush across the United States southern border on a nightly basis. It is now estimated that the United States is currently home to 12 million illegal immigrants, a population that is larger than many countries in the world.

It is evident that modern civilizations decay much faster than their predecessors because modern information technology and transportation have become catalysts that enable a faster osmotic transformation of a society from advanced to mediocre. Cultural differences within human races will always exist and the osmotic transformation will always be there to level out the differences in standard of living between neighbors unless the neighbors are equally capable, as in the case of the United States and Canada. I cannot foresee the day people living in poorer countries will become so conscientious of the defects in their culture that they would take up the challenge to abandon unproductive behaviors such as corruption, mental and physical laziness, and make a decision to transform their countries to become as good as those that they admire and want to immigrate to for a better life. I believe that poverty is not necessarily the absence of material wealth but of the ability to manage available resources.

Think about what will happen if selected number of people with the same economic status and living in the same neighborhood are given a certain amount of money, enough to open a small neighborhood store, without telling them what to do with the money, except that they would be required to give an account of what they did with it in five years time. At the end of that period, we may find that some of the recipients have made more money with the amount given to them. Another group may have bought things that they think they needed and provide a list of things they spent the money on. There may be a third group of the recipients that may not be able to give a complete account of what they spent the money on. That explains how inequality comes to exist amongst human beings. Inequality is nature's design that we cannot emotionally wish away or redress by becoming frustrated and resentful of those who do better with what they have been given. The best way to reduce inequality is by using the old wisdom of teaching a hungry person how to fish instead of giving him a free fish every time he feels hungry.

As long as a people lack the ability to manage available resources, they will continue to behave according to the law of osmosis, which would cause a society with a higher concentration of wealth to decline until it reaches the same standard of living as the societies from whence come its immigrants or end up midway between the two unequal societies. A satirical film made by Luke Wilson titled "Idiocracy" provided a good visual depiction of what the United States will look like with time. It is a film I am sure the so-called minorities (non-white Americans) may not be happy to see, and Whites who see it can only shrug their shoulders because there is nothing they can do to change the situation. That's the destiny of all human civilizations. The best we can do is to try and slow down the decline by prudent policies that may also mean putting our insatiable appetite for economic expansion under control. Unfortunately for America the stone has already been tipped over the cliff, and is now on its way to the bottom. In case anybody has forgotten, it is a lot easier to destroy things than to build them, or to do bad things or nothing than to do good things. Consider how many 9-11 terrorists it would take to build the airplanes and the Twin Towers they destroyed in a few minutes, assuming that they have the knowledge and resources to do so. To replace all the lives they took on that one day is impossible, no matter how you look at it.

11. HOW IMMIGRATION AFFECTS OPPORTUNITIES FOR BLACKS

It is possible that many black Americans, their leaders, and other activists have not given a thought to the effect a large number of Hispanic immigrants with high birthrate will have on the political and economic future of black Americans. For now, black American leaders and activists spend most of their time blaming Whites for all their problems, and appear to be speaking for black, brown, and yellow people. Frustration caused by nature has left them subconsciously wishing that white people disappear, and at the same time renders them incapable of imagining who is going to take their place, and whether the replacement would be better or worse. They seem to forget that they have been living together with Whites in this country longer than any other group except for Native Americans. Black Americans and Whites understand each other because they have been culturally associated for centuries. There are more intermarriage between black Americans and white Americans than between black Americans and any immigrant groups such as Mexicans, Asians, etc. In fact, intermarriage between black Americans and Mexican-Americans and Asians are practically non-existent; the three groups do not interact socially. If two Americans, one White and the other Black, with exactly the same level of education and economic status were to go anywhere in Latin America or Asia in search of a bride, the white American will definitely be the first choice for the women in those parts of the world, even among those Latinas classified as "morena" (a light skin woman that may even trace part of her ancestry to Africa). The only groups of Latin American immigrants that may be able to relate to black Americans are probably those from countries that have large population of people of African descent, where the influence of African culture still exists. Even then, there are still cultural barriers between black Americans and black Latinos to be considered. Even though the influence of the American civil rights movement has reached many Latin American countries, if you ask a light-skin Latino with visible African physical features about his or her ancestry, he or she will name off all the European sides first with the African side being thrown in as the last. Yet, white Americans did not put them up to behave that way and have nothing to do with it, in all honesty.

It is possible that the situation would have been different had the black race been more advanced than all other races. Regardless, I think that people should be free to identify themselves as they choose, be what they want to be, associate with who they want to, and describe their skin color as they wish. Since we all have accepted the wisdom that people should not be judged by the color of their skin, race, or national origin, but by the content of their character, it is not important how a person chooses to identify himself or herself.

The important thing to bear in mind is that you cannot force people to like you if they see no reason to do so naturally, and nobody should go through his life begging others to like him. Every individual is a complete entity and can survive in that regard but because human beings are social animals we prefer to associate with others provided that the relationship is respectful and results in a positive feeling for all involved. Whether people like you or not should not stop you from going about your life doing the best you can to be a decent person, provided that they don't go out of their way to prevent you from doing so. But I believe that all decent people are rarely disliked by those who come in contact with them regardless of race, religion, or national origin.

It is worthy of note that while black American leaders and activists constantly speak of black and brown or rainbow coalition in their demands and protests against white America, no such words are used by Hispanic and Asian leaders and activists. Obviously, black

Americans are oblivious to the fact that Hispanics as well as many other non-black immigrant groups avoid interaction with black Americans socially, and only occasionally ally with them when it is convenient to them. After all, human beings tend to lean towards or identify with whoever they perceive to be the winner. Mexican-Americans and black Americans constantly clash in California high schools, the prison systems, and on the streets, but during his second Los Angeles mayoral campaign, Antonio Villiagosa, a Mexican-American, made a great deal of effort to get the black politicians on his side in order to defeat his white opponent. However, as soon as he was elected the mayor of Los Angeles, he began talking about Mexico and California having a special relationship. The essence of the special relationship is that the mayor welcomes more Mexicans to come into California, with a chance of increasing his Hispanic political base. I imagine that five years from that election, he may not bother to try and win black voters to his side because the Hispanics can easily elect him, regardless of how Black, White, and Asian voters might vote. Tribal voting pattern is very strong among Hispanic voters.

The concern is that Hispanics may not have the same willingness to negotiate issues as Whites do and may not institute or maintain any special programs for minorities amongst them, if they take control of any states, cities, or the whole country. As currently the case, any demonstration by black Americans against any Hispanic run administration in the United States, regarding civil rights issues, will be countered by Hispanic demonstrators; whereas, the White leadership usually invites minorities to sit down and discuss the issues. The reason may be a combination of cultural mentality and the fact that Hispanics have been categorized and treated as a minority group, and benefit from programs that should have been reserved only for Native Americans and black Americans. There is a difference in cultural mentality between the Hispanics and Whites, which may not allow them to tolerate opposition as Whites might. There is going to be a rough road ahead for black Americans as Hispanics begin to take control of many cities and states across the United States.

While black Americans heavily vote for the Democratic Party, they seem to over look the fact that it is the same party that supports large scale immigration from Mexico and Central America into the United States. As the large scale immigration continues unchecked, it will eventually render black Americans politically irrelevant.

12. BLACK AMERICANS AND POLITICAL ALLIANCES

I have always been perplexed by the fact that black Americans always vote overwhelmingly for the Democratic Party. I was a teenager in Nigeria back in the early 60's when the first black American student to be admitted to the University of Alabama, James Meredith, was prevented from entering the University to attend classes. Mr. Meredith was personally prevented from attending class by none other than Mr. George Wallace, the Governor of Alabama. Governor Wallace's reason was not because Mr. Meredith did not have the right grades but because of his race. Nigeria had just gained its independence from Great Britain a few years back. Many Nigerians as well as people in other black African countries felt very bad about the incident. I followed the story with a great deal of interest in Nigerian newspapers because it affected me so much. I could see myself in Mr. Meredith. It turned out that Governor Wallace was a Democrat, but so was Robert Kennedy, the Attorney General, who confronted the Governor head-on over his refusal to allow a black student to enroll in the University of Alabama. A similar incident had played out a few years earlier in Arkansas, which caused the Republican President, General Eisenhower, to take a similar measure as JFK did in Mr. Meredith's case.

In reaction to the incident, Mr. Meredith was offered a scholarship by the Nigerian government to study in a university there. Years later, Governor Wallace apologized for his racist behavior and was promptly forgiven by black Americans. Why was he quickly forgiven? He was a Democrat. And what do Democrats do? They pander to minorities by tacitly making them believe that they cannot compete and, therefore, the bars should be lowered to enable them to get positions they would otherwise have to work very hard to achieve. They also make it easier for minorities to get government benefits, and they also want the immigration door left wide open. It does require a special caliber of human beings to say to the Democrats, "No, thanks, I know I can do it on my own, and I will" or "I don't think that such a policy is going to help the United States to keep its status as a first world country." The Democratic Party can truly be described as the party that is willing to give this country away to any group that cries, complains, or threatens. If anyone believes in reincarnation, he or she may consider the present Democratic Party as the ghost of the one that was defeated in the Civil War to free the slaves and keep the country together, but now back for revenge against the United States of America. Strangely enough, it has enlisted the help of Blacks, Hispanics, Asians, immigrants, and even some poor and middle class Whites to help it accomplish the mission.

Now, let's flip the pages of history back to the civil war. Over 600,000 Whites, Blacks, and Native Americans died in that war, which was fought mainly for the freedom of the African slaves while keeping the country united. On the side of freedom of the slaves was the Republican Party led by Abraham Lincoln, and opposed to the freedom of the slaves was the Democratic Party. This most important milestone in the history of the United States of America is what makes me wonder why black Americans are so blindly dedicated to the Democratic Party today. What was the big sin of the Republican Party that greatly outweighed the Civil War history and caused such a lope-sided shift to one party, the pro-slavery Democratic Party? The civil war was well documented and not an oral history that could have easily been forgotten or distorted. I still feel tears every time I watch the Civil War documentary made by Ken Burn. Could the reason be that the Democratic Party now offers material things and easy success to today's generation of black Americans? Or is the party telling black Americans that it understands they cannot make it unless the bar is lowered, as opposed to the Republican Party saying, "I don't see you to be any less than anyone else, you can make it but you have to try"? Modern living is full of attractive material temptations but have these suppressed honor, pride, and dignity? Black Americans still accuse white Americans of past injustices, but the worst of all the injustices was slavery followed by segregation and discrimination. But isn't it odd that in spite of their strong feeling about slavery they still feel comfortable allying with the very political party that represented the worst in the history of slavery in the United States: the opposition to the freedom of the slaves?

If the Democratic Party had really repented and felt ashamed of what its predecessor stood for, and now want to be forgiven by Blacks for its terrible history, its first step to start the healing process would have been to change the name of the party. But oddly, it still keeps the name in spite of its awful history. I cannot understand how Blacks can protest certain words that they consider as having racist connotation but don't see anything wrong with keeping the name of the political party that historically symbolized slavery, which represented the darkest phase in the history of this country. Anybody who has the ability to close his eyes and visualize himself as one of the enslaved ancestors during the period the Civil War was raging on, and realizing who was fighting and dying so that he could be freed and who was fighting and dying so that he could be kept in slavery, would be able to feel some tears of admiration for those fighting to free him, unless he has totally lost all feeling of what it means to be a human being. Many Blacks are even opposed, with very strong emotion, the presence of the Confederate flag in any state facility, but the Democratic Party, which can be described as the architect of the Confederate flag is embraced with both arms. What an irony and a confused state of mind!

I believe that only through sacrifice can anyone achieve true honor, pride, and dignity. Once the civil war ended and the emancipation of the slaves was proclaimed, true emancipation could only be achieved by Blacks themselves as free people. Allowing themselves to be bequeathed, for whatever reason, to the same political party that was opposed to the freedom of their ancestors for material gains does not look like true self emancipation for a people that are cognizant of the tremendous suffering their ancestors endured. While I have no illusion that a poor and hungry person may not be able to reject food for honor, pride, and dignity, I expect educated black men and women to look at political and social issues based on well thought out logic.

I pray that black voters do not heed Obama's call during his reelection campaign to vote for revenge. Obama did not say what the revenge is all about. Is it revenge against society for the kind of childhood he wished he could have had but didn't? His childhood was not typical of a normal American child of white, black, brown, or yellow race. It's my belief that a civilized person will only pass on a pleasant experience and throw away an unpleasant one. We should show others a better way to treat one another when we are in charge instead of repeating the behavior that we didn't like when we were at the receiving end. Revenge or retaliation only perpetuates a seesaw behavior which passes on conflicts and enmity from generation to generation. It doesn't make us a better people than those we seek to take revenge on. It was even strange that Obama was urging Blacks to take a revenge on the political party that has historically accumulated plenty of credits for fighting for the freedom of those before them or their forefathers while letting the real culprit off the hook.

There was a documentary film, shown on PBS, about a reunion between the descendents of a Southern slave owner and the descendents of his slaves, where a young black descendent was asked some question along the line of if he feels lucky to be here in America considering how bad things are today in black Africa. My thought as I listened to the question was that if I were to answer the question for him, I would have said, "Well, let me pretend that one of my ancestors were sitting right here and I could relay the question to him by asking if my being here in America is a fair trade for what he went through. His answer would be my answer." I don't think that any human being would volunteer to be someone else's slave so that his offspring could have a better life, nor would anyone wish that his parents become slaves so that he could have a better life in the future. Could the later be the case today where Blacks seem to be sacrificing freedom, honor, pride, and dignity in order to acquire easy material gains? Come to think about it, those past black men and women who fought for the freedom and dignity for their people seem to be mentioned less and less nowadays because they spoke about honor, pride, and dignity. How often do we hear about Frederic Douglas, Booker T. Washington, and Martin Luther King Jr. these days?

The pattern of voting for several groups of American voters is now beginning to look eerily like the tribal voting pattern common in black African countries, which prevents those countries from electing capable and honest leaders. Everyone votes for the politician from his tribe regardless of how corrupt and incompetent he is, and sometimes, the tribes clash over accusation of election fraud, as was the case in Kenya a few years back, which resulted in the death of over 1000 people. In the Middle Eastern countries, the voting pattern is based on religious sects. It is now firmly established in the United States that liberals, Blacks, Hispanics, and Asians, as well as those receiving benefits from the government, will always vote for the Democratic Party even if that behavior sinks the country to the bottom of economic sea figuratively. On the other hand, the conservatives seem to still hang on to the freedom to vote or not to vote for a Republican Party candidate because how they vote would not cause them to lose any benefits if the candidate fails to win the election. Sometimes, the fear of losing legitimate benefits from the government under a Republican president is simply unfounded, but the tribal voting mentality has taken root and has become hard to undo.

Another issue of interest is that black America has become open to any group that is willing to ally with it politically with no consideration whatsoever for cultural or traditional compatibility. A case in point is that of what Rev. Jesse Jackson used to refer to as Rainbow Coalition, which means he is representing or fighting for black, brown, and yellow people." NAACP and other black leaders, including those that marched with Rev. Martin Luther King Jr., have now declared that same-sex marriage issue is recognized by them as a civil rights issue, comparable to the Civil Rights movement by black people whose ancestors were brought to America as slaves, and a civil war had to be fought to free them. The declaration came on the heel of President Obama's declaration of support for same-sex marriage. Black people occupy a huge chunk of a continent, which is their land of origin. I wonder if the same could be said of Gays and Lesbians whose ancestors have never been traded as commodities, except for the Blacks amongst them, of course.

It is unfortunate that in the desire, among many Americans, especially black Americans, to elect the first black president, they had grabbed the first thing that glistered without checking to see if it was really gold. Once the initial mistake had been made, there was no going back. Going back would have backfired terribly against the Democratic Party and its followers. So, they are willing to do whatever it takes, including sacrificing the very country they live in, to prop up Barack Obama. Blacks are even willing to stomach the kind of insults they would not tolerate from a white politician if they come from Barack Obama. An example was his cajoling of Congressional Black Caucasus (CBC) during the healthcare legislation debate to "stop whining, stop complaining, stop crying, and get out there and fight." He wanted them to go out and confront the Tea Party protesters, even if such a confrontation could have led to violence. Many of those men and women in the CBC have been in the civil rights movement before Obama was born and in politics while he was in college.

While Obama was visiting Ghana, he told Africans that their countries have been independent long enough, and they have no excuses now for not moving forward. There was no adverse reaction from the black African leaders nor did African presses challenge Obama on the statement. That would not have been the case had George Bush made a similar statement whether at home or abroad. Criticism would have been swift, emotional, and vigorous from black leaders, activists, and social justice warrior journalists right here in the United States. On the contrary, during his campaign speeches to his political base, mostly college students, Blacks, Hispanics, Asians, and the so-called poor and middle class, Obama did not cajole them to work harder to make their lives better; instead, he told them that the odds against them were so overwhelming that they need government help to make it through life, under his presidency.

He would take from the successful Americans and give to the poor and middle class. He labeled that "fair share" or "fair shot" in his political speeches. Yet, he is not sharing the glory of winning the presidency because he constantly reminds his opponents that he won the election; therefore, it should be his way or no way. More than any other president in the history of the United States, his statements are full of I's, me's, my administration, and my White House. That is not the behavior of someone who believes deep down that he worked real hard to earn what he has. Only a person who conned or lied his way into something displays that kind of behavior because he does not want to let down his guard and be discovered for who he really is. Most accomplished people in the world let their actions and achievements speak for themselves. They don't go around trumpeting them or waving them in people's faces. What people sometimes perceive as arrogance or elitism may actually be an attempt to hide a deep rooted feeling of complex. You can see how that is linked to Obama's invention of characters and events that did not occur or rearranged them to suit his purpose right from the time he was a young boy to this day. After all, other animals are known to use loud noise to scare off much larger would-be adversary.

Whether Barack Hussein Obama was fathered by a foreign student from Kenya or an avowed black American communist, he did not grow up as a mainstream black American. Having been born in Hawaii, he spent part of his childhood in Indonesia and later embraced the idea of being the son of a Kenyan foreign student who grew up herding goats. If that is the true story of Barack Obama, then he doesn't fit the historical punch line that we all have been looking forward to, which is a descendent of an African slave rising to become the president of the land that enslaved his ancestors. Even if Obama is proved to be the biological son of Frank Marshall Davis, the avowed black American communist, his family background still doesn't represent that of a typical black American. Obama and his supporters may celebrate his eight years of aberrant occupation of the United States presidency, but that may well be like a house built on a faulty foundation. When the faulty foundation eventually gives way and the dust settles, Obama may well leave a legacy of the first black American president who presided over the decline and fall of the United States. I hope that those who have contributed, celebrated, and benefitted from Obama's eight-year aberration will be honest and courageous enough to own the giant misstep that sent America off the cliff. What will politics be like if black Americans find themselves with a country of their own to run, should the United States break up? Has anybody given that possibility a thought yet?

13. IS AMERICAN MASS COMMUNICATION WAR A PRELUDE TO CIVIL WAR?

Journalism in the United States used to be the source of news and other investigative reporting that people looked upon to provide them information regarding what is going on in the country and elsewhere, whether the events were public or private, as long as they were important to the society and relevant to people's lives. With the advent of the internet, journalism has become a weapon of mass abuse of all kinds. It seems like all people need to do nowadays to become journalists is simply arm themselves with a computer and an access to the internet. The result is that people now appear to be soldiers sitting on trenches and foxholes waiting for the enemy's head to pop up so that they can start firing. Mass media of today fosters the proliferation of hatred, and licenses people to vilify, and possibly destroy the character of those that do not share their viewpoints. The anonymous nature of "web journalism" has brought out all the hidden viciousness and hatred that we could not imagine that American culture could produce. Social media has been used in every vicious manner possible, and I suspect that just like any other addiction, it may someday escalate to physical violence among the hitherto verbally warring groups.

A sign that journalism has lost its original goals of observing, investigating, and informing the readers and listeners is that when the so-called minorities and liberals decide to study journalism these days, it appears that they literally see themselves as cadets entering a military academy to study the art of warfare. Once they are in school, they are only interested in studies that train them to fight against those they perceive to be the enemy of "their people" or those opposed to their political and social ideology. They are not interested in text books with balanced view of the social issues facing society; instead, they read text books that reinforce the prejudice with which they entered the journalism program. They seek out only those professors that are radical enough for their purpose. Very few of them, if any, ever consider concentrating their studies in subjects that would enable them to bring helpful information to the community they consider theirs and encourage the people to abandon negative behaviors and become better armed in pursuit of success and a better life. They see themselves as warriors in some undeclared racial and social justice war.

Once they are out of the journalism program they join the rank of minorities and other progressive liberal and radical journalists who constantly vent their frustrations and resentment against other human beings, mainly conservatives and white Americans. Come to think about it, what are they going to do with the white women after they have disposed of the now hated white men? I suspect that they would probably do the same thing barbarians in ancient times were known to do when they overrun a civilized society – carry off the women into captivity. I hope that the Democratic Party and its followers don't end up forcing tribal mentality on Whites also, because that is not going to be good news for America. Now, the list of enemies has increased to include successful or well-to-do Americans based on a relentless attacks initiated by the American nightmare of Barack Obama's presidency.

In an attempt to keep the culturally incoherent "rainbow coalition" that was the winning ticket for Obama, the Democratic Party has inadvertently turned on white Americans, who are now vilified openly on a daily basis. To watch white liberals even lead the way in the vilification and condemnation of their own race irrationally is strong evidence that America has gone over the peak of its civilization and now on its way down. Could the United States have existed if the Pilgrims from England didn't come to settle this land for religious freedom? Have liberals, progressives, social justice warriors, and every other group within the Democratic Party "rainbow coalition" ever wondered where they would have been and what they would have been doing today if the Pilgrims didn't make it? It appears that liberals of all stripes are progressively losing their sense of rationale at an unbelievable pace. They have now convinced themselves that the only good Whites, Blacks, Hispanics, Asians, etc on earth are those that go along with the Democratic Party, the historical party for enslavement of Blacks, in its determination to fundamentally transform the United States. That party of enslavement is now at it again, but this time it has garnered the support of culturally incoherent groups, including the group that it fought hard to keep its ancestors in slavery, and leading a crusade against white males and anyone else that disagrees with it. It reminds one of the kind of campaigns that took place in the former Soviet Union and China during the communist revolutions, which preceded the physical elimination or internment in re-education camps of their own citizens. First, you have to demonize those that are opposed to your ideology in order to energize herds of supporters to embark on the execution of your devious plan. I would imagine that once they are finished with white males, they will probably turn on independents of all stripes. Then, finally, once the common enemies are gone, it will be time to turn on one another. Makes you wonder sometimes what human beings really are, and if they are as intelligent and rational as they claim to be. How do you explain the wrong turn into the direction of self destruction that this society has made?

There is no evidence that these racial and social justice warriors are ever going to be able to recognize that nature is really responsible for who we all are as individuals or collectively as a group. They could have been like the people they are condemning and attacking but for nature's design. It's nature that made us black, white, brown, or yellow. It's nature that gives us abilities to do well in various fields of endeavor in life. Some of us are better thinkers than others; some of us run faster than others, some of us work harder than others, etc. What we are in life is all based on what nature equipped us with. If the ratio of talented individuals within a racial group is higher than in other groups, more people within that group will naturally be successful. It was all set up by nature. So, why can't racial and social justice warriors accept the truth and try to figure out how to help those behind catch up rather than pull those ahead backwards? The answer is that nature is a headless thing; you cannot talk to it, you cannot complain to it, you cannot stage a protest march against it, and you cannot throw rock at it. All you can do is use whatever it gave you to try and survive its harshness. Besides, it requires discipline, dedication, and a great deal of efforts to catch up than to complain or try to destroy those perceived to be doing better.

You can see that all the restrictions put in place by nature, such as inability to do things that would make us successful, can create a great deal of frustration in people. However, since nature is beyond reproach, the frustrations are vented against those around us that appear to be relatively better off than we are. This kind of frustration is interwoven with envy and some elements of defeatism, all of which are irrational behaviors. The racial and social justice warriors should be able to remind themselves that white people have got only one head like everyone else, and that, perhaps, cultural behavior is what has helped them to become more successful than others that live in the same society. The successful people against whom racial and social justice warriors vent their frustration were born the same way as everyone else.

Many of them have gone through some difficult times to achieve anything worthwhile in their lives. It may even be liberating if the racial and social justice warriors could put aside their frustration and false pride and conduct interviews with several successful people of all races and ethnic background to find out how they got to where they are. If they could bring themselves to do this kind of interview and then let their communities see how people succeed, there could be hope for a peaceful future for America. However, experience has shown that the easier thing to do is to constantly attack, vilify, criticize, derive and demonize those that are successful, out of frustration, envy, and resentment.

The situation in the United States is slowly turning into what the Israelis have been experiencing in the Middle East. Prior to the creation of the state of Israel, the Jews were a powerless minority in Palestine; they had no voice and the Arab Palestinians weren't bothered by the presence of poor Jews. That changed when highly educated and highly skilled Jews from all over the world settled in Israel after its creation. Within a very short time Israel became the most developed, democratic, and modern society in the Middle East. For the rest of the world it stands out like the proverbial shining city on the hill, but for the Arabs, Israel is a source of shame, a sort of sore thumb in reverse, figuratively, because all of its Arab neighbors that have been there for centuries still remain much less developed and less democratic than Israel. If the Arabs had accepted the creation of the state of Israel at the end of World War II, and became good neighbors, they would have benefitted from the expertise the returning Jews brought with them; instead, they became envious and resented the presence of Israel and set out to destroy it. The same frustration-generated envy is now manifesting itself in the United States where minorities blame white people for all their ills. Those ills are put in place by good old headless Mother Nature, but the frustration has to be taken out on other human beings. If the Arabs didn't set out to destroy young Israel, perhaps, Israel wouldn't have made conscious efforts to block the osmotic equalization of its society and those of its Arab neighbors, especially the Palestinians. The two societies would have lived peacefully side-by-side with little difference in their standards of living as a result of osmotic equalization. If the Palestinians ever decide to live peacefully as neighbors of the Israelis, the Jewish state and United States may someday end up looking very much alike. They will both become mediocre developed countries, except that the United States may get there faster, judging from the current war being waged against it by the racial and social justice warriors and other radical progressive journalists. By the way, when the United States is taken down several notches, Canada will not escape the same fate because of the osmotic equalization. Then the sipping will be going from Mexico and the United States into Canada until its standard of living drops to the level of its neighbors.

14. SOCIAL JUSTICE VERSUS EQUAL JUSTICE

The ideology of social justice is more like a wolf in a sheep's skin. I think that some group of people somewhere that was frustrated by the failure of communism decided to repackage the failed harsh anti-nature ideology and label it with a more religious sounding name. But as the saying goes, no matter how you dress up evil, once the surface is peeled off, it is still going to affect all that it touches in a bad way. Social justice in plain language believes that when we are born, we are all equal and, therefore, should have the same level of mental and physical abilities. So, for social justice proponents, if some of us somehow manage to become more successful than others, we must have done something wrong or unjust and the situation must be redressed by redistributing the success to the less successful.

Beyond the "if you have a business, you didn't build that" philosophy recently introduced into American politics by leftist radicals and made popular by Elizabeth Warren and Barack Obama, social justice proponents haven't really explained how and why one person does better in life than others, even when they were born twins and raised by the same parents. Social justice, as a "humane" ideology, believes that the results of successful efforts by some people in the society must be taken forcefully and redistributed to those who are unable to obtain good results from their own efforts or did not put in enough efforts. To the social justice proponents, charity cannot be substituted for forceful redistribution. I believe that social justice is a defeatist ideology wrapped together with human envy. The frustration-generated envy can be traced to Mother Nature's design. Social justice ideology is based on emotions and cannot be supported by any rational thinking, because nature is responsible for the situation that it seeks to correct.

Powerful kings used to confiscate lands and levy taxes on their subjects to build palaces and monuments for themselves, but there are no such kings in the world today. Their role as landowners and tax assessors has been taken over by modern governments. Under social justice ideology, it is the government that levies taxes on successful citizens and redistributes the proceeds to the poor and those that are less successful. Social justice or redistribution of wealth will definitely cause the economic health of a society to deteriorate. As people realize that they can easily receive a steady free assistance from the government, they will most likely stop making reasonable efforts to improve their lives. That means that you will have less people who are interested in working. Similarly, those whose incomes are redistributed to those who now have no interest in working will stop making efforts to create more wealth that the government would snatch up and redistribute. The result will be a significant decline in productivity and downward spiral from an affluent to poor society.

Contrary to social justice, equal justice is universally accepted because it is a belief that everybody is equal in the eyes of the law regardless of their station in life. The most important aspect of equal justice is the protection of those members of the society who are not rich and powerful from those who are disposed to intimidate or bully others. Every society should be dedicated to the achievement of equal justice, so that those who commit crimes are punished regardless of whether they are poor or rich and powerful.

The American justice system has come a long way from the days when a black man used to be lynched for touching a white woman in certain regions of the country. In some of those incidents, the law looked the other way. Those dark days of the United States system of justice is gone. However, it is not uncommon these days to hear complaints about black men being locked up in jail disproportionately than any other groups. The Hispanics are now right behind blacks in that arena of social reality in America. Why is it that the population of black Americans is over represented in the prison system? Again, we must look into culture and nature that produced it. Remember that culture is what dictates everything we do; therefore, changing a people's cultural behavior requires dedicated, deliberate, and persistent efforts on the part of the people themselves. While the efforts are concentrated on the young, adults should also be constantly made aware of what is positive and what is negative. I believe that a free intelligent people should be able to look at themselves and determine what they are doing or not doing that leads them to fall behind other groups in the society. It is not enough and, in fact, counterproductive to mold your culture into that of a protester against policies and ideas originated by others.

We now have a new expression, black-on-black crime, in American vocabulary, but black politicians, psychologists, sociologists, journalists, and religious leaders are yet to get together and establish a special national institute that will dedicate its work to cultural re-education of black Americans. If they make good progress, we will see the end of black-on-black crime. The work of such an institute may become a model for other groups all over the world. Some black activists have the habit of telling Whites that they cannot understand black people, even though they, the black activists, claim to understand white people. Yet, the same activists turn around and blame whites for not doing anything or not doing enough to solve problems in the black community. If the black activists understand the black community, as they indeed should, then why are they not coming up with the reasons for the existence of the problems and detailed plans to solve them? If Whites cannot understand Blacks, as the activists claim, how do they expect Whites to solve the Blacks' problems? The fact is that it is easier to accuse and complain against others than to own the responsibility for what is wrong and make dedicated efforts to find a solution, especially the one that involves change in cultural behavior.

Unless, enough effort is expended by blacks themselves to change certain aspects of their cultural behaviors, blacks will continue to be over represented in the United States prison systems, even after the country may have attained a perfect equal justice for all. We can all agree that it would be ridiculous for police to go knocking on the doors of white Americans and taking people who are sitting in their living room watching TV to jail in order to make up quotas for white Americans in jail because they could not find enough Whites to arrest in the street.

15. THE ELECTION OF BARACK HUSSEIN OBAMA

We will examine here why Barack Obama succeeded in America beyond his wildest dreams. It wasn't long ago that many Americans and businesses would receive letters from some Nigerian scammers requesting the recipient's bank account to deposit some millions of ill-gotten dollars in their bank account. The scammers invariably claim to be princes, sons or relatives of a traditional ruler or chief, belong to a family with oil fortune, have relative in high position in government, etc. Then they would concoct fantastic stories of imaginary oil deals or huge government contracts that resulted in a huge sum of money waiting to be grabbed, which they would like to transfer into the bank account of the recipient of the scam letter. Usually, they would ask for some upfront fee to enable them to bribe some government officials to expedite the fund transfer. It always turned out to be a scam and many Americans lost thousands, if not millions, of dollars in the scam known as Nigerian 419, named after the Nigerian government decree against the worldwide scam.

Some suggested that those who fell for the scam did so because of their own greed. However, I believe that the main reason was lack of understanding of people from the third world countries. Many Americans do not understand the cultural mentality of the people in the third world countries and the level of corruption in those countries and how it works. They also tend to see people from the third world countries as humble, unsophisticated, and innocent. There is no doubt that a lot of immigrants from the third world countries can make great hosts when you go over to their home for dinner, but that should not deceive anybody into thinking that the same behavior would translate into honesty and efficiency in a workplace or in a business setting. If those scam letters had come from Americans, the recipients would have either ignored them or reported them to law enforcement. However, the recipients were willing to give the foreign scammers the benefit of the doubt.

Barack Hussein Obama definitely did not appear to be a normal American once he told the story of his goat-herding father from far away Kenya. That sure made him exotic and different and a man with a humble beginning who probably appreciated every inch of America. From then on everything he said was not subject to verification. After all, America was dying to have the world, especially the Muslim world, see us as a country of everybody. America was ripe and ready to fall into the palm of someone like Barack Obama. Besides, the country has been going through some softening process for a long time. For decades, the agents of decline, including radical professors in American institution of higher learning, liberal newspapers, liberal politicians, liberal journalists, civil right activists, immigration right activists, gay and lesbian right activists, and leftist trade unions have been at work chipping away at the country's foundation one brick at a time. While the reasons and objectives of these different groups may not be exactly identical, the end result is unmistakable - the decline of the United States of America. They are intentionally or unintentionally sending America downhill because complacency has numbed people in this country to the point where they do not see danger in the policies promoted by these groups. They cannot see nor imagine the danger in uncontrolled immigration or the gradual but steady destruction of the moral fabrics of this country and the people's religious beliefs.

What happens to a society when its moral fabrics and religious beliefs are discarded? The people can do anything, if it isn't against any law made by man, which, too, may be discarded in due course when it is perceived as becoming an impediment to unrestricted lifestyle. Within those agents of decline, there are some that are truly convinced that they are moving on to the next level of American civilization. Those call themselves the "Progressives." Then there are those that ideologically see America as a big bully that needs to be cut down to size. A third group may comprise of people who are frustrated and envious of those they perceive to have it all, and are convinced that they are never going to get there. For this last group, their conviction is that they would have nothing to lose if the whole thing called America is destroyed.

Let's now go back to Obama's life as a child. First, Obama believed that his father was a foreign student from Kenya who herded goats as a child. That was the story he told in his 2004 Democratic Party convention keynote speech, even though it was possible that Obama may have known that his biological father was Frank Marshall Davis, the man he referred to as "Uncle Frank" several times in his autobiography, Dreams from My Father. Frank Marshall Davis was an avowed black American communist, as described by Joel Gilbert in his documentary film, "Dreams from My Real Father." However, sticking to the more exotic story of a Kenyan goat-herding father appeared to have worked the miracle for Barack Obama. I doubt that Obama would be willing to submit to a DNA test to confirm who his real father was. In the same flowery speech at the Democratic Party convention, Obama claimed that the "ideals of the United States was represented by the American Flag draped over his father's coffin." Remember that the assumed Kenyan father never stayed in the United States and became an American citizen after his studies in Hawaii and Massachusetts; instead, he returned to Kenya where he began writing papers promoting socialism there. With the anti-colonial fervor and the heightened sense of nationalism during the early 60's it was inconceivable that a Kenyan who believed strongly in a socialist form of government would be buried in his country with the

American Flag draped over his coffin. To Obama, none of that mattered, he needed to fit in the "America, the Beautiful" narrative to make the listeners believe that he really appreciates this country, even though it would be very hard, if not impossible to find another American politician that matches the resentment he harbors for the United States of America.

Psychologically, Obama had developed the habit of making up stories about himself from a young age. He may have started out that way to make up for the good family foundation that he lacked. That enabled him to fit in whatever environment he found himself. Since the stories had always been about places that Americans know very little about, they have been accepted without a challenge. So, making up stories for an audience that he believes would not bother to verify them became a habit for Obama. In other words, Obama became a pathological liar as a means of fitting in and getting ahead. Obama has turned out to be a great masquerader and a very successful one at that. Some people may say, "Well, that's what politicians do" and I challenge them to produce a politician in this country that matches Obama's background and character. Proofs of made up stories and non-existent characters abound in his autobiography, Dreams from My Father. Unfortunately for the country, by the time investigative journalists and historians began to probe deep into Obama's background and the stories in his autobiography, he had already been elected the president of the

United States. At that point, both the Democratic Party and his backers in the mainstream media would do whatever it takes to prevent the exposure of Obama as a liar and a masquerader. Such exposure would have also caused enormous damage to the Democratic Party and Obama's mainstream media supporters. Those cover ups have now been carried forward into a second term for Obama, as the president of the United States. The Democratic Party is hoping that by the end of the second term, they would have given United States citizenship to millions more Hispanics and Asian illegal immigrants and pulled millions more so-called poor and middle class Americans into government dependency. With such overwhelming numbers of grateful constituents on its side, the Democratic Party is not going to bother with how Obama had conned the American people into putting him in the highest office in the land.

The result of the 2012 election has exposed two common third world cultural behaviors now taking root in American political system. One is bribery, such as exchange of cash or other form of favor for votes. The other is the tribal voting pattern, which requires people to vote only for people like themselves. The later has been very much alive among Hispanics and Blacks. It is very likely that Asian Americans will follow the tribal voting pattern as more Asian Americans run for public offices. In the recent election, they went with Hispanics and Blacks for the free handouts and wide open door immigration policy dangled by Obama and the Democrats. The Hispanic and Asian Americans want to be able to bring in more relatives and friends, and see those already in the United States illegally given amnesty. Once they receive the amnesty, they want to be able to dump them into taxpayers care.

Obama and the Democratic Party have demonstrated that anybody can be accepted into the social welfare system without questions asked. Many immigrants bring their parents to the United States after providing proof that they are financially able to take care of them. However, once the parents get their residency or citizenship, they end up getting benefits from the government to which they have not contributed because they have never worked a regular job in the United States. Besides, with improvement in Chinese economy and more freedom to travel, many Chinese now travel to the United States as tourists and students, but not very many of them return to China. Votes account for why the Democrats are never excited about reforming the social welfare programs to weed out fraudulent applicants and those that are not qualified. Either way, it added up to an incentive to vote for Obama and the Democrats. For black Americans, the fear of being asked to go out and compete with everyone else or take up the challenge of advancing their own community to the point where they can earn the admiration and respect of others seems to be the major reason for remaining attached to the Democratic Party.

Barack Obama's election was good and bad depending on how you approach the historical event. It was good for all the groups that want wide-open border and easy welfare system as well as progressives and other radical groups with more sinister motive of fundamentally transforming the United States of America. Obama is an active proponent and a spokesman for all those groups.

The election was bad for Obama because historians now have a bench mark for the decline and fall of the United States of America; in fact, Obama couldn't have showed up at the worst moment to become the first black president of the United States of America. Besides, he is presiding over the imposition of European socialist and social justice systems on Americans with century old tradition of individualism. Democrats and all their leftist allies may be tasting blood because of an election that was worn by the kind of fraud and bribery that are reminiscent of elections in third world countries, but I would caution them not to get carried away or erroneously believe that such a dubious victory could be used as a mandate to blatantly ram more unacceptable leftist agenda down the throat of American people. After all, the election illustrates the reason why the founders intended the country to be a republic instead of a democracy. They envisioned that somewhere along the way some individual or group is going to come up with a fraudulent scheme to win an election, and then use the result to impose their will on a minority or even a silent majority group. The Affordable Healthcare, otherwise known as Obamacare, showed how winning an election in a democracy can lead to the imposition of unfair and oppressive law on a silent majority.

What happens to a country where a powerful drug lord or dictator goes around poor neighborhoods handing out cash to the people in the street? Of course, the recipients would sing his praise, but the recipients and the country now belong to him and are his to do with as he pleases. For certain, there is not going to be a shortage of revealing books written by people from inside and outside Obama's administration once he leaves office. Those books will no doubt leave a bitter taste of Obama's presidential legacy in the political taste bud of the American people. I hope that the Republican Party and honest hardworking Americans will not allow the Democratic Party to disown the crisis and rioting that may be in America's future. Any serious minded person should expect problem if this or succeeding government runs out of money and can no longer fund the freeloading fiesta. When such a massive bribery is used to win an election in a country, that country's political system is broken, and it will take a miracle to bring the system back to a true democratic system without significant upheavals.

16. OBAMA AND UNINFORMED YOUNG VOTERS

As observed previously, Obama had developed the ability to make up stories early in his life and because his audience never challenged him, he realized that he could say anything in a speech and gets cheered whether the points he is making are factual or not. Obama grew up believing that the average American will swallow anything he is told about far off places hook line and sinker. He had realized that the young people are even more vulnerable. He has observed that they are so distracted that they would believe anything without considering its validity. After his return from Indonesia, he found out that his schoolmates and other kids had no idea where Indonesia is and what life was like over there. So, Obama literally had the cheese and the knife in his hands and his schoolmates had no choice but accept whatever slice he cuts and hands out to them.

Considering Obama's family background, he must have seen young Americans as living a privileged and carefree life compared to his own life and the life he has seen in the foreign places he had lived or visited as a child and as a young man. The foreign students he hung out with in college had also reinforced his own experience about the disparity between the life of American students and that of their counterparts in the third world countries. This has permanently created a strong resentment against the United States in him. Evidence of these resentments abounds in Obama's speeches at different stages of his life up until the time he began running for public offices, and even further sugar coated some more once he was put up to run as the president of the United States. That was when his speeches began to include praises for the United States as a great country and the constitution as a great document. However, during his campaign for the presidency, the resentments he harbors for this society occasionally slipped out, such as his statement that America produces five percent of world energy but consumes 25 percent, accusing Americans of not speaking French and other foreign languages while they expect everyone else to speak English, his redistribution of the wealth statement to Joe, the Plumber, the statement about people in places like Pennsylvania hanging on to their guns and religion and afraid of people that don't look like them, describing the United States Constitution as a document full of negative liberties, and many others that can be found in print and on videos. Several videos exist also showing Obama on tirades against white people and rich Americans. Obama and his wife both became "proud" of their country once he was nominated as a Democratic Party candidate for the United States presidency, which is what you might call a fair weather patriotism, but prior to that, they made a staunch anti-American couple or, at least, were steamed with resentment for the country and the supposed white power structure that has run it since its founding.

Young Americans do not search for political or philosophical information or discussion on their own except when it is a required course in college, and they usually pay just enough attention to get their grades. Even then, the textbooks they read terribly paint a one-sided picture of this society because liberal and radical professors select the textbooks that they agree with for general education courses. On environmental studies, the professors look for textbooks they agree with, and those are always the ones that condemn the United States for excessive consumption of everything on earth. It is, therefore, not surprising that young college students will blindly follow someone who tells them what they want to hear, even though that person deeply resents them, their parents, and the very country in which they hope to find a career, have a family, and live till their old age. It is the ultimate con and deceit that may only dawn on them many years later. It's like a replay of the era of the hippies and love generation, except that there are added incentives now for this generation: government will take care of all their needs. Obama represents the Pied Piper of Hamelin to young American voters.

17. THE AMERICAN EDUCATION SYSTEM

For a country that other countries look up to, American high school and college students appear to be more ignorant about public issues and world affairs much more so than their counterparts in other parts of the world, including the third world countries. That was the group of voters that were constantly targeted by Obama for political speeches that were full of inaccuracies because he had learned from his college days that most American students don't pay attention to domestic political issues and foreign affairs. If the young people are to be able to fit into the global world that we live in today, there need to be changes in high school and college curriculum to teach American history, civic duties and responsibilities for young citizens and residents of this country. They should understand the American system of government and compare it to other forms of government around the world. Students have to know what kind of political and economic systems the United States has and how that created the opportunity that attracts a larger number of immigrants to this country more than any other country. Unless young Americans understand their country and its government and economy, they are not likely to understand the required qualifications for political offices, and why they chose to vote for a particular candidate. By understanding the society they live in and how it functions politically and economically, they will not be voting for a candidate because he appears "cool" or looks like them.

It is a well known fact that many American institutions of higher learning are now stacked with extremely liberal professors whose goal is to churn out the next generation of zombie liberals. Even prior to getting to the university, young high school students have already been initiated into the brainwashing process by members of the powerful teachers' union. Many high school students, especially the minority students, are indoctrinated with the tribal mentality in the so-called ethnic studies, even before they reach college. To expose the young people to a balance general education, it would be necessary to have textbooks that present all sides of the political spectrum, allowing students to understand both liberals and conservatives viewpoints. After the students have been exposed to the two sides of the argument, the rest is up to them to figure out which way to go as they leave school for the real world.

For inner city high school students, it will be very important to start including technical education in the school curriculum by establishing well-equipped workshops that would teach the students of both sexes different kinds of technical skills. Acquiring technical skills in high school would not only reduce the dropout rate but will also help young people with their career decision. Young people with technical skills are rare in inner city Black and Hispanic neighborhoods, and yet millions of Americans who fall into the middle class use these skills to get there and not by virtue of a college degree. They either learned the skills from trade schools or acquired them on the job. Apart from learning enough technical skill to become self-employed, students who leave high school with these skills may be employed in various companies. Private companies are always disposed to donate equipments that would be used to train the students so that once they leave school they would not need much further training to become productive. The exposure to technical education in high school may help young people to choose their field of studies in college. Besides, if you can't invent or build things, you should learn how to repair things because that is an indispensible skill to have and will enable you to make a decent living. This country cannot afford to be churning out young people that have been brainwashed in ethnic studies from its institutions as well as those with bloated student loan debts they hope may be exchanged for votes.

18. THE REINVENTION OF A GODLESS WORLD

This country was founded by Pilgrims who were persecuted for their religious belief, and wanted a place where they could worship freely. To ensure that the state does not dictate what religious denomination citizens belong to, the constitution was written to separate religion from the state. However, the belief in God was never an issue; for that reason, the word God was freely mentioned in the constitution and declarations by the founding fathers.

I think that some words about the universe will be in order in this discussion about what is happening to religious belief in the United States. The beginning of the universe has been extensively discussed in the past amongst theologians and scientists. While theologians believe that the universe was created by a Devine power, God, who is inexplicable by humans, some scientists believe in the big bang theory as the origin of the universe. The scientists have so far not been able to prove their theory and are, perhaps, still working on it. If they succeed in proving how the universe came to be and that God has nothing to do with it, then some people may be convinced to go along with a Godless America. Others may still hang on to their belief in the existence of a Devine Power. The theologians have never pretended that they could go into the laboratory and set up a test to show the existence of God, so the onus is not on them. As for me, I think that the side of the theologians is safer. First, there is an expression that says that if you don't believe in something, you will fall for anything. The idea that there is some power we may have to answer to later for the way we lived on earth brings some moderating effect into our lives. Secondly, if we rid ourselves of all kinds of fear of a Devine Power, we may lose what really makes us human and may see a return to the age when man was a savage roaming the earth like any other animal. The reason is that religion was actually born of human intelligence, and consequently gave us morality.

The universe is incomprehensible to human beings. Nobody knows the extent and the shape of the universe and what else it contains besides the planets and other heavenly objects we have been able to identify through the telescope. If the "big bang" theory was true, and the universe is expanding spherically, is it expanding into an existing space or creating space as it expands? Does anybody know if the universe will continue to expand infinitely? If it does not, what forces would cause it to stop? If it stops expanding, would it collapse back to what it was? If it stops expanding, but does not collapse, what forces contribute to its equilibrium? In case of equilibrium, has anybody figured out what is on the other side or the boundary of the universe? Another universe, may be? I doubt that anyone alive on earth today, including those that are newly born is going to get the answers to those questions in his or her life time. The result is that human beings will never abandon their belief in the existence of an invincible power that created the universe. This is the reason why every society, civilized or not, has a name for God. As humans advance in science and technology, their attention is diverted to material things, and the search for the origin of the universe, and questions about how we come to be, who we are, and the purpose of our existence, or if our existence should have any purpose in the first place, all get pushed aside. Therefore, while we advance technologically, there is no parallel progress in the quality of human beings. In fact, it appears to be going backwards as society evolves into freedom without fear of God or any sense of responsibility. Perhaps, this would not have presented any danger if all human societies had developed in unison and passed through the same experience to get to that level of freedom. The disparity in development among humans acts as a built-in generator of conflict. As the quality of human beings deteriorates, so will our relationships with one another.

Our belief in God comes from our inability to understand the universe. We see God in the forces of nature that we struggle to live with the very first day we are born. We can tell that the earth went through some turmoil during its existence. The evidence of the turmoil is everywhere and continues to present new challenges to our existence. Whether you believe in the theory of evolution or creation, it is undeniable that a great deal of turmoil or violence took place before the earth came to be. To a large degree, we have come a long way in our struggle to survive the forces of nature, even though we cannot conquer or control nature. We will always live with these forces. This makes me wonder, sometimes, if humans will ever know real peace, since the earth came to be through tremendous turmoil. We are a part of the products of the violence that brought the earth into existence. Is it possible then that humans can ever overcome this violence inherited from nature? One can argue that with the intelligence that we have developed or has been granted to us, as humans, we should be able to shade that violent part of our nature. Unfortunately, we still harm and kill each other because we are unable to reach a point in our civilization where we are able to discard bad experiences and pass on only the good ones.

The belief in God and organized religion has moderated human behavior. Of course, it is easy to cite instances where people have been killed or oppressed in the name of religion, but those few instances are outweighed by the good religion has done. The idea of loving your neighbor as you would love yourself or treating others as you would like to be treated did not originate from man-made laws; it came from religious teaching. Charity, the act of helping others in need was never decreed by any government or man-made law; it came from religious belief. The movement to end the slave trade was spearheaded by the

Christian Churches. The famous Underground Railroad movement, which helped slaves to escape from the Southern States of the United States to the North where they became free, was organized by Christians based on their religious beliefs.

After the British Parliament abolished the slave trade, the British Navy was ordered to sea to search and seize any ships carrying slaves, and set the slaves free. When the British Navy captured slave ships and freed the slaves taken from the coast of West Africa they had to be taken somewhere and cared for. By the time those slaves were loaded on the slave ships and out to sea, they may have been in captivity for months. For people who were village dwellers, there was no way they could have found their way back to their villages. They had to be settled somewhere in West Africa similar to the environment they came from. The British government could not take that responsibility but the Christian Churches did. They helped the freed slaves to construct new dwellings. Schools and clinics were built by the missionaries where the freed slaves were taught how to read and write, and health services were provided to them. Two famous black West African missionaries and educators, Bishop Samuel Adjai Crowther, and Dr. James Aggrey were the products of the work of the European missionaries.

When we help the needy or do good deeds there is a subconscious feeling that a higher power is watching us and will reward us either here on earth or in the life after. You can't find many people that wouldn't like to die with a smile on their face symbolizing satisfaction that they are departing life without any regrets because they haven't done bad things in their lives. For someone who is about to die, that peaceful feeling is based on the belief that there is another place or experience awaiting him after death. That is belief in the existence of God. It wouldn't hurt anything if we go through life with the fear that we will be punished, after we die, for any bad thing we do in our life.

   If we abandon religious beliefs, treating and loving others as you would like others to treat you would be out the window, and the word charity may be erased from our vocabulary. It may become pretty much a no holds bar world with thousands of nuclear weapons sitting around. Without spiritualism our main concern about whatever we do and the way we live our lives will be based on whether there is a police watching us. The idea of hell and heaven will seize to exist. Our punishment for whatever man-made law we break will be received here on earth. The word conscience may no longer have meaning because it is based on the subconscious feeling that some power is aware of everything we do. If our wrong doing is not in the law book, then we are home free, nothing to bother our conscience. If there is no law against watching other human beings suffer or allowing something bad to happen that you could have prevented, you wouldn't feel guilty. If a society succeeds in declaring all rules, whether of laws or morals, as impediments to freedom and, therefore void, then anything goes in that society.

However, it does not look like the scientists are going to present a proof of their theory of non-existence of God any time soon, because, I imagine, they may need to accumulate extensive amount of data from other places in the universe for analysis, before they can arrive at a conclusion. I suspect that the attempt to prove the evolution theory may even be abandoned as time passes since human beings do get bored with whatever they are doing. The argument about the existence or non-existence of heaven and hell is not as important as the belief that they exist, because that is what contributes to the moderation of human behaviors. If we believe that they don't exist, then we will lose that moderating effect.

Human beings are not perfect and nothing they build or do will be perfect either. As human beings, religious people fall within this restriction imposed on us all by nature, but they strive to produce more positive results in their lives. People pray to overcome the bad side of their nature, so that they will be able to live a more beneficial life. We may be putting the world at a greater risk by seeking to wipe out religion in people's lives. If we succeed in doing so; it may take just the next generation of humans, who believe in nothing, to turn on itself and self-destruct.

I am convinced that those who are pushing a world without God and religion are not only shortsighted but also selfish. If we reinvent a Godless world and destroy religion, we may have the freedom to adopt any lifestyle we desire without worrying about criticism from those whose religious beliefs are opposed to that lifestyle. However, as the rule goes, nature abhors vacuum; something is bound to replace God, religion, and morality as a consequence. As we all know, changes and revolutions often produce undesired consequences. Everything we do may become subjective to each individual and if individuals that see things in a certain way get together in a group, they may decide to act to rectify any situation they are opposed to using any means they consider necessary without fear of repercussions. That is possible if human beings are completely void of any conscience.

Without religion, we would not have had basis to develop a sense of morality, and it wouldn't have been possible for us to feel obligated to make laws to protect the individual freedom. So, no matter how we look at life, we just cannot eat our cake and have it too. We just can't foresee what we are going to get when we discard religion and the morality it teaches. As you push for reinvention of a Godless world, remember the advice: "Beware of what you wish upon yourself."

19. NATURE ASSIGNS WHO WE ARE

Slavery was an unfortunate and terrible part of human history, but its existence was the result of the unequal mental development or lack of the exercise of mental ability among human beings. Cultural advance is a product of the mental development of a group. I rank slavery next to cannibalism on the scale of man's primitivism; in fact, many may prefer death to slavery. Logs from slave ships' captains showed that many slaves from the Ibo tribe of Nigeria would jump overboard, at the first opportunity and drown in the sea rather than survive the trip across the Atlantic as slaves. Slavery also portrayed how uncertain human beings were and still are about the real meaning of civilization. I see equality as a human idealism that is not supported by nature. Based on that, I strongly believe that you cannot enslave someone who is more knowledgeable or more advanced than you are, because one of two things could happen in that case. One possibility could be that the enslaved person will soon be teaching you things that would force you to set him free.

At the end of the World War II the Allies grabbed any German scientists they could lay their hands on; some of them ended up in Russia, but majority of them chose to give themselves up to the Western Allies. Those were the scientists that developed Hitler's deadly war machines, including the German rockets, but regardless of which side of the Allies that grabbed them, they were not put in prisons to punish them for developing Hitler's weapons of war, instead, they and their families were made comfortable and put to work for the country they ended up in. They were not segregated or discriminated in any way.

Both the United States and Russia gained from the knowledge of the German scientists.

The other possibility could be that you are so envious or afraid of the intellectual ability of the enslaved person that you would want to eliminate him for good. Although the Israelis are not enslaved but are surrounded by the Arabs, nevertheless, their situation represents an example where a group wants to eliminate another because of their apparent intellectual abilities. That is the threat looming constantly over Israel. The existence of Israel as the only developed and democratic country in the entire Middle East puts all the other countries to shame. It is a case of wanting to exterminate a race of people out of envy. While Israel is still less than 70 years old, the rest of the countries have been in existence for centuries; yet, they have not been able to create one true democratic and developed modern society. The modern structures in some of those countries can be classified as having been bought with wealth from petroleum resources. If foreigners didn't discover the oil that was buried deep beneath the earth, it would have remained where nature put it forever, and there would have been no modern infrastructures anywhere in those countries. I always imagine that if for any reason the oil boom comes to a screeching halt some day, it may take less than 20 years for those oil producing countries to begin to look like a civilization-gone-by. The Arabs didn't mind when Jews were a powerless minority in Palestine and other Middle Eastern countries until highly educated and skilled Jews returned from various parts of the world following the reconstitution of Israel.

How some people become more mentally developed than others is a subject that has been tacitly tabooed in today's world for fear of the usual emotional racism outcry. Political correctness has instituted a new unwritten law, which says that truth is evil, a sign that the world we live in is heading down the slope because we are living on false pretext. It intrigues me that while we accept and talk about physical differences amongst individuals within a race and within different races, we avoid the mention of mental and cultural differences from the discussion. We organize beauty contests all day long and select models to advertise the products we make all day long, yet we shy away from that which is the most important to human survival on earth, our mental ability. Cultural and mental differences are, indeed, what separate groups that have made greater technological and cultural advance than those that are trailing behind. Mental difference only separates one individual from another within the same group as well as across groups. In other words, individuals who are intelligent can be found within any racial group. If a racial group happens to have a higher ratio of intelligent individuals within it, in combination with positive cultural behavior, that group is likely to make more significant contributions to the advancement of mankind, in general, than other groups.

I believe that the differences in mental ability amongst the various races or groups can be attributed to the environment in which each group evolved or existed. If the assumption that humans first evolved in the African continent holds, then it is obvious that the groups that left the continent earlier and faced harsher environments might have developed better mental ability in order to survive the harshness of nature. That agrees with the wisdom that practice makes perfect. This further led to the development of better nutrition and environment that encouraged invention and modernization. Unfortunately, those that live in parts of the world where a lot of modern inventions had not taken place tend to continue to sit back and make no efforts to invent something new or make further improvements to the inventions of others. That is to say that they have accepted the status quo, which means that there is no need to make efforts to develop the ability to invent new products or ideas. Of course, there is no need to reinvent the wheel, as the expression goes, but if you don't have something inside that challenges you to master the use of the already invented wheel and use it diligently to make your life better, you are going to be left behind feeling sorry for yourself and complaining about life. The Japanese are said to have taken apart the inventions of others and redesigned better products from them.

When Barack Obama told Africans during his visit to Ghana that they have no more excuses for not moving their countries forward after so many years of independence from colonial rule, he wasn't wrong but there were a whole lot of implications to that statement. Easier said than done, I say! Obama and every black person everywhere in the world ought to be challenging themselves everyday based on that statement to those in the African continent. I challenge Obama and many other people who may be frustrated by what they see as social injustice to search inside themselves for answers as to why the world is the way it is, and who set things up that way. If they do, they may come to the realization that other fellow human beings did not really set up the world to favor one race or the other. That realization may, perhaps, enable them to dissipate the frustration, resentment, and anger they may harbor for other human beings and instead begin to challenge nature. It was Mother Nature that set things up the way they are, but nature also gives humans intelligence to do what they can to fight against it in order to survive where other animals may not. Animals become extinct because they don't have highly developed intelligence to survive the environment in which they found themselves.

So, Obama was actually talking to himself as well as to black people everywhere when he told Africans that they have no more excuses for not moving their countries forward. Except for a few countries, almost all the black African countries became independent in the early 60's, a mere fraction of how long it has been since the end of slavery in the Americas. Based on his statement to Africans, doesn't it occur to Obama and his fellow social justice warriors that the same statement could apply to black Americans and Latinos considering that slavery ended over a century ago? The position black Americans occupy in this society, in relation to other groups, can be described as analogous to the one occupied by black African countries with respect to the rest of the world in general. However you look at it, black people on both sides of the Atlantic seem to bring up some rear of some sort respectively.

Would it not be in order to expect that any group of people that have creative energy bursting out in their veins could have risen within that period of time to compete with all comers in the society? The story of the enslavement of Jewish people is older than Christianity but when they were freed, they didn't exactly take the back seat; and they haven't been extinct either, in spite of the Egyptian Pharaohs and Adolf Hitler. Instead, they have thrived and have been contributing in many fields of human endeavor, and the most important of all, they didn't do it by being specialists in protests.

The fact is that we have failed each other on both sides of the Atlantic. If the Africans had risen from colonization and showed the world that they have what it takes to move the continent forward, similar to what the Japanese did at the end of World War II when they found their country in ruin, I have no doubt that they would have salvaged the image of black people across the Atlantic. They could have inspired people of African descent all over the Americas and the Caribbean. They would have provided black Americans with a viable argument that it was slavery that suppressed their creative energy. I suspected that just the emergence of several black African countries from colonial rule to independence in the early 60's, with voting rights in the UN General Assembly, probably brought some sense of urgency into the passage of the Civil Rights Bills in the United States Congress.

If the situation was reversed and the creative energy of black Americans had surged once they were freed from slavery, then Africans could have blamed their situation on colonization. Of course, it may be a harder argument for the Africans to make for a people that did not even have any writing and no cities before the arrival of the European colonialists. You can tell what people had and knew historically by those things that they have names and words for in their native languages. Consider that the only country that has functioned relatively well as a modern society in the African continent is South Africa, a place originally settled by people from Holland seeking religious freedom, just like the Pilgrims, and later joined by other settlers from England, which eventually colonized the country. There is no denying the fact that every racial group has been endowed with certain talent by nature or through cultural practices. However, such a talent may not be enough to lead a group to equality with others in this modern era of technology, so the group must learn those things that did not come out of their cultural experience and then pass the knowledge down to the new generation. Remember that the Japanese really did not develop any formula that anyone 60 years or older studied in school or anything that anybody can put his finger on. But because they are highly disciplined and conscientious people, they were able to take apart the inventions of others, studied them, and then designed better products.

20. THE CONCEPT OF EQUALITY

I would imagine that the concept of equality began to take root in human societies with the development of philosophical thinking by the Greeks when they began to discuss the concept of democracy in human society. But the concept of equality is only a human idealism, a kind of utopia, because it is not supported by nature. Look around the earth and see how many things, even within the same species, that are exactly the same in every respect. Seeds planted in the same soil do not grow to exactly the same height, do not develop exactly the same number of branches, and do not produce the same number of fruits. Our body parts are not even symmetrical; for example one arm could be longer than the other, so are the fingers and the toes, and the calf of one leg may be bigger than the other. In the case of the later, would you then cut a chunk of flesh from the bigger calf and throw it away or sew it on to the other leg in order to make them both symmetrical? The fact is that nature does not permit such a modification without a price. Sometimes, the price may be a simple scar, but sometimes the result may be fatal.

If equality is supported by nature then all people would have acquired the same physical and mental attributes from nature, and all societies would have progressed at the same time, and to the same level. At the time Europeans were outfitting ships and sailing across the oceans, Africans, Asians, and Indians in the Americas would have been doing the same. The relationship would have been one of equal and mutual respect. Trading would have been in goods, and colonization and slavery would never have happened. When we go to school, each student pursues the field of studies he or she is interested in and most comfortable with. However, some fields of studies may lead to a better career success than others. People pursue certain fields because that is where their natural interest and ability lie. This is an example of how inequality evolves among human beings.

What we all have in common are all the human emotions, which are responsible, in various ways, for the human conflicts that exist everyday and everywhere in the world. Among all the human emotions, pride and shame are, perhaps, the two that lead to all the conflicts because they breed resentment, envy, anger, frustration, and revenge. Frustration may be caused by our inabilities, failures, and mistakes, and may lead to anger and envy towards those who are perceived to be doing better. People who are frustrated by nature tend to generate conflicts or start fights easily. They vent their frustration in form of anger, verbally and physically, and it does not matter that the recipients of the anger really did not create the circumstances that led to the frustration.

Frustration is the work of nature or circumstances put in place by nature. People who are not frustrated by human inequalities are not easily angered. Those who are frustrated by their own inabilities, and unable to compete with others, are also likely to be impatient and less persevering. They tend to give up at the very first attempt at doing something complicated, if they failed. The point I am trying to make is that individuals and groups are doing exactly what nature put them up to do; blaming others for their failures and inabilities is a sign of frustration. Frustration causes people to become irrational and violent. Frustration put in place by nature is linked to envy, which is the major contributor to terrorist attacks against the United States and the West. Even some parts of the world that is not known to breed terrorists may quietly welcome the attacks based on natural envy they have for the country that is the target of terrorist attacks. Frustration and envy prevent us from learning from those who are the subject of the envy.

The concept of equality as it relates to human beings is really abstract. Respect, on the other hand, can be earned. Most of the time when people talk about equality, they are actually referring to respect. We may never be equal but we can respect one another and live happily together. There are several character traits that can bestow dignity and respect on an individual or a group in the eyes of others. A cultural behavior that would teach a person never to take anything that does not belong to him no matter how dire his situation is would definitely earn respect for that person. Once in a while we read about a taxi driver or a homeless person who finds lost large sum of money or other valuable object and returns it to the owner. That display of honesty is always admired by majority of the people in the society; however, there is no doubt that there are a few unscrupulous people who may see that kind of honesty as a stupid act.

If you see an old lady coming towards you in a quiet street and you feel that she might be a little nervous with fear that you might snatch her purse, and instead of thinking to yourself, "That's her problem, I am not a thief" you simply cross to the other side of the street just to assure her that you are of no threat to her. That gesture may well teach her not to be afraid of the next person she sees that looks like you. You move into a nice quiet apartment or neighborhood and determine that you are not going to alter the status quo. Your new neighbors will accept and respect you. In fact, anytime you prove to people how wrong they are about their misconception of who you are, without having to confront them verbally or physically, you will not only earn their respect but may have earned the same respect for other people that look like you. Even behaviors such as keeping your neighborhood extremely clean and crime free would make everyone else want to live in that neighborhood regardless of the race or color of the people that live there. What I am getting at is that regardless of whatever special benefits the Democratic Party gives to black Americans and other minorities or whatever bar it has lowered so that they can get in the big chair, the real respect and admiration is going to come from those things they achieved by their own talent and efforts.

21. IMMIGRATION TO THE UNITED STATES

In a world that has been made literally very small by modern information technology and means of transportation, it is easy for people in other countries to see how Americans live and decide that they want to come here to have a better life. Proximity affords people from Mexico and Central America the easiest opportunity to come into the United States illegally. They see no hope that things will improve soon in their countries under the present culture of corruption, mismanagement, and inefficiency. These behaviors seem so rooted that only a miracle can change the status quo. And so, the immigration to el Norte continues to be a logical option to living a life of poverty and frustration.

Much has been said about the United States being a country of immigrants, even though all the three countries that make up North America have similar history of colonization by Europeans: United States by Great Britain, Canada first by France followed by Great Britain; and Mexico by Spain. Canada, like the United States has received large number of immigrants of late, but Mexico is the only country whose people are emigrating out in large numbers. Due to proximity and easy access, Mexico leads any other country currently in the number of illegal immigrants entering the United States. However, with recent economic improvement and more freedom to travel, the Chinese may be able to overtake the Mexicans in a few years; all they have to do to accomplish that is get one percent of the population of China in here. Mexico could have been a country of immigrants too, rather than a country of emigrants but for its inability to develop its society and economy like the United States and Canada.

This issue is never brought up in the illegal immigration debate because it will lead back to the question of what is wrong with <u>Mexicans</u>. You notice that the word Mexicans is used instead of Mexico. This is to call attention to the fact that it is the people that make a place or country what it is and not the things that are put in there by nature, such as the soil, the trees, and the animals. Remember that poverty isn't necessarily the absence of resources but of the ability to manage the available resources. Unfortunately, it is no longer politically correct to bring up this kind of question in the immigration debate. Even in academic discussions, it is a taboo in this charged atmosphere of political correctness for a social scientist to study such a subject and publish his findings. The real reason is that any attempt to explore this question would lead back to nature. Nature is something that we cannot accuse of discrimination, call names, or force into making things right by creating special programs and quotas. Instead, the frustration created in

Mexicans by nature is blamed on its northern neighbors, if they do not want to let Mexicans into their countries or feel sorry enough for them to let them stay, if they manage to get in illegally.

A great part of human behaviors is instinctive; for example, immigrants know they can find job in the United States and have a better life. So, they pack up their bags and off they go to the United States in search of that dream. Once in the United States, they find a job and start making more money than they ever dreamt of in their country of origin. However, the question of how the United States made that possible where their country of origin couldn't is never contemplated. Without the philosophical consideration of the how and the why, the immigrants are most likely to hang on to the cultural behaviors of their country of origin. You would also think that once the immigrants become part of the United States, they would appreciate the society and resolve to avoid those behaviors that have not been beneficial in the society they left behind. Unfortunately, things don't turn out that way. Once they have their foot in the door, so to say, the next thing most immigrants do is to proclaim pride in the society and culture they left behind and began to align with the political party that literally accepts them as they come without any requirement to assimilate culturally. It isn't uncommon to hear a newly naturalized citizen make a reference to the country he left behind as his or her home right after he stepped out of the courtroom where he or she had just sworn an oath to defend the flag and constitution of the United States against any enemy, and uphold the laws.

Americans who were born in this country may also not contemplate the possible adverse impact to this society if immigrants are not assimilated by teaching them to adopt American language, culture, and way of life, rather than keep the cultural behaviors of their country of birth intact. Some Americans may see these strange cultural behaviors as sort of exotic and harmless, and rarely think about the cumulative effects on this society.

Relevant government documents, such as those for voting, driver's license, and government managed benefits are now translated into Spanish and several other foreign languages for immigrants. You can see how the United States has been gradually creating nations within a nation, and inadvertently encouraging immigrants to recreate the ills of corruption, mismanagement, and inefficiency, which were rooted in the societies that they came from. This has been going on now for decades and cannot be reversed. The situation was caused by lack of vision on the part of the politicians and people of the United States that watched it happen while shrugging their shoulders. It has now led to the tribal voting pattern by Hispanic voters in the United States, who now vote overwhelmingly for a Hispanic councilperson, state legislator, congressperson, or presidential candidate, when he or she shows up, even when a White or a Black Democrat is the opposing candidate. The immigrants seem to forget that the countries they left behind were and are still run by Hispanics, like themselves, and that perhaps, they may one day find themselves feeling like they are back where they came from.

In a recent oath taking ceremony in one of the three venues in Southern California where about six thousands new citizens were sworn to oath, I observed a very interesting behavior exhibited by the new citizens. During the welcome speech given by an official of the United States Citizenship and Immigration Services (USCIS), she announced the top five countries of origin of the new citizens as Mexico, followed by the Philippines, El Salvador came in third followed by Vietnam, and China was the fifth. The official counted backwards from the fifth, China, to number one, Mexico, and the interesting thing was that as she announced the countries, the new citizens from each country applauded. If you had a decibel measuring instrument at the ceremony, it would have literally blown off the scale when she got to the number one country of immigrants to the United States, Mexico. What intrigued me most was why it is a source of pride for the new citizens to be ranked so high as the people that abandoned their country of birth for another country. By that display, it would appear that those people believed that they have made it to paradise, having escaped from hell. But don't swear to that because it was possible that once they stepped out of the temporary courthouse, they were back to being proud Mexicans,

Filipinos, El Salvadorians, Vietnamese, and Chinese. They have gotten their feet in the door now and it's time to be their true selves.

I doubt that there was a Japanese immigrant at the ceremony, even with the level of natural disasters that the Japanese people face constantly in their country. If there was, I would suspect that true love and marriage may have been the possible motive. The reason is that the discipline in Japanese culture has produced a highly dedicated and less corrupt people. Japanese products are practically part of the life of every human being everywhere in the world today. The Japanese people are respected everywhere in the world because they have earned it. Without being asked, even the then apartheid government of South Africa classified the Japanese as honorary Whites, so that they wouldn't be segregated from white South Africans as other so-called colored people and black South Africans were, as required by the apartheid system of government. Today, the Japanese people have no need to leave Japan to find a better life elsewhere. Earlier emigration of the Japanese was related to the turmoil caused by the end of feudalism in that society. Wherever they went, they have taken their cultural discipline with them, which enabled them to contribute to the progress of their new country. Brazil is said to have the second largest population of people of Japanese descent outside Japan. They are respected Brazilians because of the positive contributions they have made to the country. The Japanese Americans who were interned during the World War II did not allow the experience to define who they are, and did not pass on any scar from the experience to the new generation of Japanese-Americans, so they could possibly use it as a subject of constant political agitations and bargaining chip for special government funded programs and benefits. It wouldn't be unreasonable to believe that if any Japanese-American voted for Barack Obama in the election of 2012, it must have been for reasons other than the hope of leaving the immigration door wide open so that they can bring their elderly parents and other relatives and then dump them into the care of American taxpayers. Any other people with similar cultural attributes as the Japanese can achieve the same results.

As an immigrant, I am perplexed by how these immigrants process their reasons for moving to the United States. They seem to want to eat their cake and have it too. Every culture has something good and bad about it. The good things about a culture determine the good results it produces, which provides the people with a decent life. For people to leave their country of birth to emigrate and become citizens of another country there has to be something in the new country that makes their lives more conducive than they were in their country of birth. The immigrants should be able to identify the cultural behaviors that made their lives less conducive in their countries of birth and leave them at the border, so to say. If immigrants are unable to identify bad cultural behaviors in their country of birth, they are very likely to take those behaviors with them and transplant them in the new country. I was old enough to remember how well my country of birth was administered when it was still a colony of Great Britain. As a young man, I had high hopes that the country was about to really take off after independence because it was our fatherland and we ought to care about it more than the colonial administrators. It didn't take long after the dust had settled from the euphoria of our new independence for me to realize that the country wasn't moving forward; in fact, it was moving backwards literally. It became obvious that the negative cultural behaviors were simply waiting for the colonial administrators to leave so that they could become the prevailing force.

Any honest observer could see that the negative cultural behaviors had no chance of reforming themselves. The situation could be described as similar to the biblical Sodom and Gomorrah, where Enoch was unable to find 10 residents without sin to save the city. When he failed to find enough people without sin, God ordered the city to be evacuated, and then destroyed it. If immigrants believed that the situation in their respective countries of origin was temporary, or if they could see hope on the horizon, they would not undertake to go on a perilous journey to enter another country. Without hope on the horizon, they take the risk of entering another country illegally; after all, we have all got one life to live, and you better live it where you feel most comfortable. My only problem is that immigrants seem unable to put their reasons for wanting to become part of this country in true perspective. If their perspective is all about having American taxpayers provide them with the better life, smuggling in more relatives and friends, replacing American cultural behavior with those of their countries of origin, and creating a tribal voting pattern in the United States, then they are contributing to the decline of their new country.

We need to consider the long term effect of uncontrolled immigration into the United States. Some of the popular arguments put forward by illegal immigration advocates are that the illegal immigrants help the United States economy, that they only take jobs that Americans don't want to do, that they make agricultural products cheaper, and that they pay taxes. Then there are activists with the slogans that Mexicans are coming to take back what used to be theirs, while others prefer to say that they did not cross the border, but rather, the border crossed them, which amounts to the same thing as saying that this is their place and that they never left it.

Let us examine the point about Mexican immigrants helping the United States economy. The first question that crosses my mind is why a person would leave his less developed country to go and help the economy of a developed country to continue to grow. Do Mexicans seriously believe that being recognized as contributing to the economic growth of the United States while Mexico is still languishing in poverty and corruption is going to earn them recognition of being equal to Americans? If American cultural behavior did not contribute in creating a system of government that led to the development of good political and economic systems, would Mexicans be coming into the United States to look for work and a better life? If Mexico has set up a well functioning system, socially, politically, and economically, there would have been no need for Mexicans to come to the United States to keep the American economy expanding, unless they are coming in as investors. The same thing goes for the issue of illegal immigrants paying taxes. I cannot imagine why anybody would leave his country, taking all kinds of risks, to enter another country just for the purpose of paying taxes, unless he sees a net gain for himself.

Usually, you have to have a social security number to be able to work in the United States, but some years ago some pro-illegal immigration legislators pushed a bill through that allowed the IRS to issue a special number that illegal immigrants could use to pay income tax. That maneuver has been used in the argument that illegal immigrants pay tax; therefore, the United States benefits from their presence. Of course, the illegal immigrants would not pay tax to the United States if they had remained in Mexico or whatever their country of origin is, because they wouldn't have the money to pay such a tax, even if they had wanted. Being in the United States enables them to pay tax under this arrangement while they are living in the country illegally. I have no doubt that the illegal immigrants have been advised that they could use the tax records to establish their presence in the country should the 1986 type of amnesty be instituted again. As it turns out, illegal immigrants that pay tax to IRS are now bilking American taxpayers billions of dollars annually in fraudulent income tax refund by claiming dependents allowances that cannot be verified by the IRS because all the dependents are supposed to be living in Mexico. It is clear that the net gain is always on the side of Mexico in its relationship with the United States and Canada, a situation no politician dares to call attention to due to the grip political correctness has on this society.

Let's now look at the activists' claim that they are here to take back what used to be theirs or that the border crossed them. Here is a good example of nature's built-in frustration. The reference is obviously to territories ceded to the United States by Mexico during the Mexican-American war. Of course, Mexico received payment for some of the territories. However, such an argument would not have been the case if Mexico had lost or ceded some territory to its poorer southern neighbors some centuries ago. Since those countries may not be doing better than Mexico, economically, there will be little benefit in making claims to such territories. Besides, it is very hard to find a piece of land anywhere in the world that has not changed hands during the course of history of mankind. The land now known as Mexico used to belong to various Indian tribes before Spanish explorers came there. Today, not many Mexicans identify themselves as belonging to any Indian tribe, which means that they, too, may be occupying land that originally belonged to someone else.

Almost all of the activists with this point of view are American born, and either their parents or even grandparents were the generations that crossed the border to live in the United States. In spite of having been born, raised, and college educated in the United States, these activists are still unable to feel equal enough to white Americans to simply go about their daily business of making a living and teaching their offspring to do their best to contribute to the society they live in, and not live the life of agitators and complainers. Somehow, they subconsciously feel that this society is not theirs because they didn't build it; they are only trying to fit into the system created by someone else. What they perhaps don't consider is that they can still contribute to making the society better or, at least, ensure that it continues to function well. By so doing, they would have earned a great deal of respect for themselves. Being a useful citizen is sometimes all that it takes to be respected by your fellow citizens. They need not look over to Mexico for who they are because they can define themselves right here in America as Americans, based on what kind of citizens they are and how hard they are willing to work to earn it. After all, their parents and grandparents came here to have a decent life which Mexico did not provide them. To try and recreate the Mexico that their parents and grandparents left behind will be a terrible irony.

We all need to guard against allowing the need in human beings to be respected and recognized as important and equal to interfere with logic. When pride comes before humility, it becomes difficult for people to ask themselves if they have earned the pride and respect they desire. Even if that crosses their mind, they realize instinctively that it may be almost impossible to earn the pride and respect they desire because it requires a fundamental change in attitude. That is when frustration sets in followed by resentment. Soon the frustration and resentment are translated into protests and violence when the opportunity presents itself. Frustration takes over because the activists realize that they do not really have anything better to offer that can surpass the system already created by those who managed this society to where it is today. The activists could have been proud Americans instead of claiming to be proud Mexicans while living in America. They cannot be denied their rights as Americans provided under the United States constitution. Of course, having Mexico as the birth place of their parents or grandparents should add to their heritage, but I expect them to fight to protect and keep the United States functioning as well as it has been when their parents or grandparents came here, if not better.

Flooding the country with illegal immigrants in a very short period of time is certainly not going to keep America functioning as it was when their grandparents first came here. Does anybody believe that America will remain safe and prosperous no matter how much problems are dumped into it? If you want to know what America will be like if it becomes overwhelmed by immigrants from third world countries in a short period of time, you should look at crime statistics in Mexico and other countries in Latin America.

You have to realize that Mexico is run by the elites, many of whom were educated in US and Europe, yet they cannot break out of the cultural box that nature has cast them into. Therefore, I am not sure that Mexicans can acquire the ability to create and manage a well functioning society simply by crossing the border. This factor also applies to any other immigrant group from the so-called third world countries that have not demonstrated the ability to create and manage a politically and economically advanced society. Having so-called democratic elections does not indicate that a society is corruption free, as the recent United States general election has shown. A country also needs to create an atmosphere of law and order before it can move forward economically. Even if Mexican activists are given the opportunity to run the territories they now claim to be theirs, as a separate country or as an autonomous state of Mexico, can they guarantee that citizens of the new country or state will not soon be crossing the borders illegally to look for a better life elsewhere? Fortunately for these activists, the First Amendment of the United States constitution gives them the freedom to vent their frustrations in whichever manner they choose, except violently, of course.

Ironically, in spite of the protection the constitution has provided to Americans and everyone that lives within its borders, it is now under open attack as outdated by Barack Hussein Obama, the current President of the United States, who sees it as a "document with negative liberties." He and his fellow Progressives see the constitution as standing in the way of their efforts to fundamentally transform the United States into a country similar to those ruled by decrees by military dictators. By the time the Progressives have issued enough decrees, a.k.a. Executive Orders, to bring in enough immigrants and pull them into government wealth redistribution scheme in order to stay in power perpetually, they would have created a trashy society that will no longer attract new immigrants. Again, you may visualize that situation by watching Luke Wilson's satirical film, "Idiocracy."

The sad thing is that generations come and go and history and experiences communicated verbally fade away in the memory of the new generations. Young Hispanic Americans may have forgotten the stories told them by their parents and grandparents about what life was like where they came from. Today, the new generation just wants the pride of being Hispanics instead of just being Americans, and don't remember or don't care to think about why their parents and grandfathers left their countries of birth for the United States. That renders invalid the argument that the second generations, and beyond, of Hispanic immigrants would fully assimilate and see themselves as just Americans and vote for candidates based on qualification to do the job.

22. UNITED STATES AND MUSLIM TERRORISTS

The United States woke up after 9-11 but didn't stay awake long enough because it has indirectly sent a message to Muslim terrorists that the country has become nothing but the biblical Tower of Babel. The country is divided and a divided nation cannot survive sustained attacks. The terrorists know that a divided country is a weakened nation and all they have to do is continue to attack relentlessly. They know that a complacent and divided society cannot withstand protracted war and will soon lose the will to fight to save itself from defeat by a group of determined ragtag terrorists. Americans, with very little exception, talk as if terrorist attacks started on 9-11, but actually, terrorist attacks have been going on for years. Like a complacent society that it has become, the United States saw the attacks as a cost of doing business in the world, and didn't want to interrupt normal business activities. The same attitude is exhibited in the issue of illegal immigration. Think about it, thousands of illegal immigrants and their supporters took to the street, some even waving foreign flags, at the hint that a new law might make it a felony to be in the United States illegally. There was not a single counter demonstration in favor of the supposed new law but, perhaps, the most intriguing thing about it was the fact that foreigners who broke the law by entering the country illegally did not blink an eye about pouring out in the street to protest steps the society intended to take to prevent future disrespect of the immigration law of the country. Even Democratic Party law makers showed up to support the illegal immigrant protesters. Something was seriously wrong with that picture! It was a troubling evidence of the state of complacency in this society to see the show of solidarity with lawbreakers by lawmakers. It was an unprecedented irony but also doubles as a proof that progressivism and liberalism are now synonymous with complacency.

Compare the protest by illegal immigrants with 9-11 where there were jubilations on several Arab and other Muslim streets around the world, but there was not a single anti-terrorist demonstration or rally anywhere in the United States or anywhere else in the world. However, demonstrators began to show up in the streets as preparations by the United States military got underway to attack Afghanistan. Was it any surprise that no one else in the world demonstrated in favor of the United States when Americans did not go out to the streets to demonstrate after 9-11? People in this country go on protest or demonstration at the snap of the finger for issues that involve race, immigration, gay and lesbian right, abortion, union rights and benefits, and lately, under the Occupy movement. In fact, anything relating to special interest groups is worth demonstrating or protesting for, but anything that affects the national interest is not worth that kind of efforts and sacrifice. Now, doesn't that make America look like a no man's land? Remember that when terrorists exploded bombs in train stations in Spain killing some 91 people, up to one million Spaniards were out in the street demonstrating against the terrorist act. Since then, I don't think that there have been many more attempts to set off bombs in that country by foreign terrorists.

Of course, nobody protested either when terrorists attacked United States Embassies in East Africa killing over 200 Africans and only 12 Americans in 1998. No motion was introduced by any nation in the United Nations condemning that particular terrorist attack, and terrorism in general. It was a repeat of the 1979 seizure of American Embassy in Tehran, which raised no condemnation in the United Nations or anywhere else. The United States did not even request a UN resolution condemning the action as a violation of international law and there was no request for sanctions against Iran and none was imposed by the UN. The United States couldn't even bare the Iranian president from attending UN meetings in New York City or giving a speech in an American institution while in the city. Hugo Chavez of Venezuela referred to the President of the United States as the "devil" while he was attending the UN conference in New York City, and was later invited and allowed to travel to a church in Harlem. If the UN headquarters were located in Caracas, Venezuela, and an American president had referred to Hugo Chavez as the "devil" in his speech, while in Venezuela, he would have had the "persona non-grata" papers waiting for him the moment he stepped outside the UN building. That may not be his only problem; his motorcade back to the airport will be met by thousands of Chavez supporters with eggs and rocks and whatever objects they can lay their hands on. That is exactly what happens to American Ambassador on a regular basis in Venezuela. Of course, I can already imagine some Americans thinking, "But Americans don't act like that; we are more civilized than that." And I say sure you are, but remember that all past civilizations were destroyed by less civilized enemies because they acted civilized to their own detriment. Perhaps, the United States perceives those who hate America and want to destroy it as children that don't know what they are doing. It seems that Americans in their complacency are teaching the world that they feel nothing and won't defend themselves regardless of what they are accused of or what others say or do to them physically.

With such intense disagreement at home over going to war against Muslim terrorists, not many countries will be willing to get involved in supporting a country whose citizens are now retreating from defending their own country. If Americans are afraid of suicide bombers, then they should expect no support from other nations. But is suicide bombing really such a new phenomenon? It has been almost 70 years since the Japanese used suicide bombers known as Kamikaze Pilots to attack Allied ships during World War II, and the world seems to have forgotten that suicide bombing is not a new phenomenon; it's an old wine in a very crudely made Jihadist bottle. The real difference is that the Jihadist bombers are not directly sent out by a government or a country that the US could retaliate against by dropping a nuclear bomb and putting an end to the suicide bombing.

Think of what might happen if a would be suicide bomber realizes that when he or she dons on a bomb belt and goes out and kills some innocent people, he or she is putting the lives of everyone in his or her family in danger. That may well be the reason why you don't see many of the suicide bombers blowing themselves up in their own countries. Instead, many of them travel to other countries as volunteer Jihadists. Pakistan, for example, arrests family members of a fugitive from law and holds them until the wanted person turns himself in. Israelis used to order the family of a suicide bomber out of their home and then demolish the home, which, I think, is a kinder approach than what might happen to the family of a Pakistani or Saudi bomber. It may sound awful to some people in the United States but you cannot live long enough to teach a barbarian charging at you the rules of modern warfare or the technique of peace negotiation.

Perhaps, suicide bombing would run out of volunteers if a bomber could come back from the dead to let would-be volunteers know that there were no 100 virgins waiting for him. Since that is never going to happen, the United States has one of two options: send the suicide-bomber volunteers to the embrace of the waiting virgins before they waste their bomb or simply give in to whatever the Jihadists demand.

What is the motivation for terrorist attacks against the United States? I am convinced that terrorist attacks have their root in human envy nudged along by a touch of sadism. When young Muslims see how advanced Western societies are, they realize that their societies have no chance of catching up with Western societies. That frustration turns them into sadists with one desire only: to destroy what they wish to have but couldn't. They may publically condemn Western societies as immoral and call Westerners infidels but that is a case of the sour grape because given an opportunity they would like to have a taste of the glamour of Western life they have seen up close or in films and movies. Remember that some of the 9-11 terrorists were caught on surveillance cameras with prostitutes here in the United States before they committed their demonic acts. For people who are supposed to have 100 virgins waiting for them in the life after, once they have carried out their terrorist attack and killed as many people as possible, they sure couldn't resist fulfilling some longstanding desire for Western women first, right here on earth. So, it's a combined force of envy and sadism that drive terrorists to want to destroy those they see as being so advanced that they have no chance of catching up with them. The terrorists are simply venting frustration caused by nature against other human beings that really are not responsible for their situation.

Those who have been critical of the United States on the wars in Iraq and Afghanistan, or the philosophy of preemptive strike against terrorists, have yet to present a list of grievances or crimes committed by the United States against Muslims or Muslim countries that warranted the attacks over the years that culminated in 9-11. The critics need to explain what policy they want the United States to adopt to satisfy the Jihadists so that they can chose peace instead of killing others. I am sure that if you ask the Jihadist their price for peace, they are going to say that they want the United States and the West to submit to the will of Allah or die as infidels.

I believed that many Americans initially voted for Barrack Hussein Obama with the misconception that electing a non-white, especially one with non-Anglo name, would make all those who wish evil on America or wish to see the country destroyed change their minds. The irony of this misconception was that the very first attempt to murder Americans right after Barack Obama had won the election and assumed the office of the President of the United States was made by a Muslim terrorist from Nigeria, a black African country. Also, it seems to me that we have lost sight of why United States Marines killed by terrorists in Lebanon went there in the first place. They went there to keep peace, and not to occupy the country or support one group or the other in the Lebanese civil war, but it did not matter to Hezbollah and their supporter, Iran.

Right after 9-11, I was shocked to read some Latin Americans' opinions on the terrorist attack that wobbled between condemnation and justification. The justification included claim that some security forces from those countries that were trained in the United States during the Cold War tortured and killed people. My response was that assuming that their security forces were trained in counter insurgency in the United States, how they applied what they learned was probably heavily influenced by their cultural behaviors, because the FBI, which is in charge of internal security in the United States, does not torture or kill anybody arrested for subversion, whether they are American citizens or foreigners. If the FBI is not torturing and killing Americans, how could it have taught security personnel from another country how to torture and kill their own people? You can only train others in something you know how to do and have had plenty of experience in doing. Remember that you can take a person out of a culture but you can't take the culture out of the person; only that person can take the culture out of himself or herself. So, any act of torture, killing, or abduction of citizens that occurred in Latin America during the Cold War was influenced by the cultural behavior of the security forces in the particular country.

The United States had a good relation with Iran during the reign of the Shah, Saudi Arabia, Kuwait, and Jordan, but did not dictate the domestic and foreign policies of those countries. Whatever happened internally in those countries was based on their own cultural behaviors, but that did not stop the Iranians from seizing the American Embassy in Tehran, when the ousted Shah was granted a visa under President Carter's administration to come to the United States for medical treatment. Remember that the United Nations did not impose any sanctions on Iran for that violation of international law. And remember also that Ayatollah Khomeini spent years of exile in France, and the Shah never shut down the French Embassy in Tehran for harboring his most powerful enemy. It seems that the world, including some Americans, are now retreating from confrontation with irrational radicalism, even the domestic ones, as shown by the street protests by thousands of illegal immigrants. We cannot have peace in the world unless everybody understands and plays by the same rules. The United States will lose if it fights brutal terrorists the same way it would fight a conventional army of another country. All past civilizations died from savage attacks from less civilized warriors that were not taken seriously when they began to chip away at the will of the society.

Today, American universities are full of learned academicians that believe that if the United States does not respond to terrorist attacks, it will all stop, and that American imperialism brought the attacks on itself. Yet, all they can produce in the way of how America brought the attacks upon itself are theories. If the United States did not push back at the spread of communism by the former Soviet Union and China, I am sure that many of the academicians might not be where they are today. Even if the United States had retained its democratic system, it would not have been as free as it is today, if she had found herself surrounded by socialist countries, no matter how small they may be. Strange enough, the very professors that preach against American economic expansionism are the same ones that want uncontrolled immigration, knowing full well that it is the insatiable economic growth that attracts immigrants rather than the concept of democracy as a political ideology. Many immigrants understand the words freedom and democracy only as tools for asylum in the United States and Canada; they will fail if given the power to protect those two concepts. These professors may not be around when the immigrant population reaches the level where the country may be run by the Hispanic or Asian immigrants or their offspring, a situation that may not permit the kind of freedom of speech they now enjoy.

In the election of 2012 immigrants voted overwhelmingly for Barack Obama and other Democratic Party candidates, but as their population increases, it is going to be seen how they will treat the white liberals that helped them to peacefully invade and conquer the United States. Worst yet, if the United States falls under a Muslim government, many of the liberal professors in this country's institutions will be looking for safety elsewhere because they will not be able to put out lecture materials that are critical of whoever the Supreme Ayatollah or Imam would be. The arrogance on the part of liberals that such event or situation will never occur in the United States is proof that history does repeat itself.

23. THE UNITED STATES AND THE WORLD

In the 60's, the United States was engaged in Cold War against the former Soviet Union (USSR) and communist China to stem the spread of communist supported by those two countries all over countries emerging from colonial rule. The United States' two major fears were, perhaps, loss of freedom and nationalization of industries and businesses in which the West had invested billions of dollars. There was also fear that if the United States didn't take action to halt the spread of communism, there could be a possibility of a communist revolution taking place right in this country. So, the United States threw a lot of resources into stemming the spread of communism beyond USSR and China. Unfortunately, its so-called partners, the supposed believers in democracy in the countries emerging from colonization, where the Cold War physically played out, were not as dedicated as the socialist and communist revolutionaries. To begin with, the so-called believers in the democratic system were generally corrupt and city dwellers who are not used to hardship. They were not willing to fight and die for what they believe. The result was that the United States had to send personnel and equipment to the countries that were defending themselves against communist subversion. But it also committed troops or military advisers to help defeat or stop the communist revolutions in some of those countries. This was the case in Korea, Vietnam, El Salvador, Granada, and Nicaragua, to mention a few. South Koreans, Vietnamese, and citizens of other countries threatened by communist revolutions should have been allowed to do their own fighting, if they really believed in freedom and democracy. But on the contrary, while the United States soldiers were fighting and dying to stop the communists from taking over those countries, the very people they were fighting to protect were busy relocating to the United States for a better life and the American dream. It was the physical presence of United States' advisers and soldiers that left a lingering impression that it was out to dominate the world militarily. But in reality, the USSR and Chinese were behind the revolutions; they provided support for them.

The United States has become home to people of all backgrounds, cultures, and races and for that reason it gives us a glimpse of how things might turn out if UN were to try and establish a kind of world government. Political correctness has come to dominate American news media and TV, no matter whether they are right or left leaning. For that reason, any kind of philosophical and objective view of what is going on in this country and in the world has to be carefully crafted to meet the political sensitivity of a "multi-ethnic" society. The reason is that any philosophical expression that exposes a true picture of some ethnic minorities could lead to protests and a disruption of normal economic activities. And so, every news media avoids reporting news or publishing an opinion that could be construed as being unfavorable to any ethnic group, no matter what kind of influence the group is bringing to bear on society. Not many people have learned to be courageous enough to stand up for America and let anybody that thinks that he or she is a racist know that if the choice is between saving America for everyone that lives in it or be given that false label, then saving America is the only reasonable choice.

America is a good example of a society that creates problems even as it thinks it is making tremendous progress today. The country has a serious disease called complacency. This is bred by affluence and pursuit of material possession. Complacency affects both the domestic and foreign policies of the United States, including immigration and ethnic or the so-called minority issues, and how it handles unfriendly nations. If you surround yourself with material possessions that make life easier, you are very unlikely to pay attention to threats from some fanatic Muslims thousands of miles away. You also will not give any thought to the effect of uncontrolled immigration into the country because you are not losing any of your material possessions immediately. Complacency has no boundary and no class; it affects all facets of society, including the academic institutions, the intelligent services, the Foreign Service, and ordinary working Americans. This explains why America never paid a serious attention to terrorist attacks over the years until 9-11. It is even becoming controversial to invoke 9-11 as a reason for any new policy or law that is intended to keep America secure.

The controversy over the planned Mosque near "Ground Zero" highlights the level of complacency in the United States. It shows that even educated Americans either have very little knowledge of the term "Jihad" in the Muslim religion or have simply cast it aside because they see no immediate danger. They have even failed to consider the reason why the Imam who will be in charge of the Mosque chose to name the Muslim Center "Cordoba House." Cordoba is not an Arabic word; it is a Spanish word, which should have led to the history of the conquest of Spain by Muslims from North Africa. Why did the New York Imam choose to name the Muslim Center Cordoba House? It is possible that he envisions a repeat of the Muslim conquest of Spain here in the United States. Cordoba was the place where Muslims built their Mosque over a Catholic Church following the conquest of the city. In the case of the World Trade Center, the Imam realizes that it would be impossible to build exactly over the space previously occupied by the Twin Towers because work had already started in a new building on the same spot, so he decided to settle for a nearby location. Those who are in favor of the "Ground Zero" Mosque are so complacent that they do not believe that the lion can don a sheep skin, even when its tail is sticking out of the sheep skin. Do they expect the Imam to come right out and let Americans know that he wants the new mosque as s symbol of Muslim conquest of America? Of course not, because that would be an open provocation, and he is not yet in a position to come out of the firestorm that would have ensued without a protracted headache.

Complacency also caused Americans to abandon the old "look before you leap" wisdom and elected Barack Hussein Obama in 2008, about seven years after Muslim terrorists killed nearly three thousand Americans in a single day. Consider that his first and middle name are Muslim names and his surname, Obama, is only one letter away from the first name of the Al Qaeda leader, Osama bin Laden, who was responsible for 9-11. At the time of the election, the United States was still at war in Afghanistan where the Al Qaeda leader was supposed to be hiding. Just the name alone would have shocked a less complacent society with patriotic citizenry into rejecting Obama the first time his name was brought up as a speaker at the 2004 Democratic Party convention. As if that was not enough, the hateful sermon from Rev. Jeremiah Wright, who was Obama's pastor for 20 years surfaced. That was followed by revelation of Obama's association with people known to hate the United States and various speeches and writings from him and his wife showing their resentment towards the United States and its economic and political system. Although Obama kept his resentment under control during the 2008 election campaign, except for a few slip ups, he wasted no time in getting right to the business of curbing America's economic and military power. His tours of Europe and Middle East during which he assured the countries he visited that America's days of being arrogant, dismissive, derisive, and unilateral actions are over. He accused the United States and the USSR of using the Middle

Eastern countries as pawns during the Cold War with which they had nothing to do. For the tour of condemnation of the United States, Obama was rewarded with a Nobel Price.

How many presidents anywhere in the world have ever made those kinds of statements about their countries while visiting a foreign country? Only the German Chancellor has ever apologized for the Holocaust and may have chosen the appropriate forum of the German parliament or the United Nations for the occasion. Turkey is yet to apologize for genocide against Armenians. An honest candidate for the United States presidency should have made it known to the voters during the campaign or debate that he held that kind of view about his country and not hide the feeling until after the election. But then, Obama's psychological makeup does not allow him to be up front about whom he really is and what he intends to do; his true self and intentions are always couched in general flowery statements. His childhood experience has made him resentful and a specialist in protest. A protester cannot be an inventor of product nor ideas because he is naturally frustrated and resentful of people who do better than him, and the protester subconsciously believes that he cannot compete against those people and win, so, he can only protest and condemn them.

After four years of watching the economic situation of the United States go from bad to worse under Barack Hussein Obama, American voters' complacency doubled down by reelecting him to another four-year term. A non-complacent society would not have taken another chance with a character like Barack Obama. What many college students and other young voters do not realize is that Barack Obama may be very resentful of them for all those nice automobiles parked in college campuses all over the United States, all of which belong to students. Neither Obama nor his Pakistani roommate and the foreign students he said he hung out with owned any nice cars while he was a college student. Just as Obama resents rich and successful Americans, he may even resent spoiled American college students more and may want to see them ride buses to school just as college students do in most countries of the world, especially the third world countries.

24. THE DECLINE OF CIVILIZATIONS

All human civilizations are destined to decline and eventually fall. Consider that humans have life span, and are not perfect either; for that reason, as we pass ideas and experience from one generation to another, they soon begin to take a different form and meaning than the original ideas. The ideas and experiences passed on to the next generation eventually wear off. With the present technological development, the changes become even more rapid. The new generation seems to have less ability to carry forward behaviors that had kept societies relatively stable and peaceful in the past. One of our greatest problems is lack of balance. We tend to think and behave in a seesaw manner. The old expression "too much of anything is bad" seems to have disappeared from our conscience. So, we have stopped rationalizing how much of anything we can do before it is over done, and start to produce the opposite result. Whether it is the issue of how much we consume, how much freedom we want, how many immigrants we can let in at a certain period of time, how big is the vehicle we drive, how much entitlement the government can provide to citizens, how much tax we can pay, and so on; any excesses contribute to the decline of society.

Those who contribute to the decline of the society in which they live rarely think about the result of their behavior in a negative way. The politicians who embark on backroom deals, take excessive earmark, and pander to special interest or ethnic groups, all for votes are contributing to the decline of society. Those whose behaviors constitute nuisance, such as making an excessive noise, writing graffiti, and trashing public places may believe they are just having fun, but they are actually contributing to the decline of society. Those who see no reason to obey the law when no law enforcement officer is present are contributing to the decline of society because they are providing bad examples to others. They need to ask themselves what kind of citizens they are or want to be. Many people are not conscientious about making the society in which they live better. They think that it is someone else's job.

Advanced societies should be conscientious about putting a system of assimilation of immigrants from underdeveloped societies in place. This is particularly important in the United States, which is the destination for most immigrants from the so-called third world countries, if it is to slow down the rate of its decline. Unfortunately, the United States has not kept up the assimilation process, a situation that I blame on political correctness and expediency. The result is that unproductive cultural behaviors from many underdeveloped countries have gradually taken root in the United States. Among these are bribery and corruption, tribal voting pattern, crime, inefficiency, rudeness, etc. Political correctness has not allowed schools to teach school children civic duties and responsibilities right from the first grade. Students from grade schools and high schools are not taught about why immigrants come to America, what the differences are between the countries from where they, their parents, or their grandparents came and the United States, and what is expected of them as Americans. Instead, they are encouraged to be proud of the very places that they or their grandparents left to seek a better life in America. Good examples are the celebrations of Cinco de Mayo and Kwanzaa none of which has any root in American history, traditional, or religious. Cinco de Mayo was invented in a Chicano studies in a university in California supposedly to provide Mexican-American students with a source of pride in their cultural heritage. It was the day, May 5th in 1862, when Mexican army, in Mexico, defeated the invading French army. It was a war that was fought in Mexico and had nothing to do with the United States and doesn't have anything to do with Mexican culture either. In the current atmosphere of appeasement and political correctness, I do not think that Mexican-Americans will like to see another ethnic group celebrate the defeat of the Mexican army the way the Mexican-Americans now celebrate the defeat of invading French army over a hundred years ago. Yet, that celebration is becoming a permanent annual commemoration in the United States, and nobody questions the appropriateness of it.

Similarly, Kwanzaa was invented supposedly as a sort of contemporary holiday celebration as Christmas and Hanukkah. It was invented again to give black Americans something of their own to celebrate, as if Christmas is some sort of ethnic holiday. Its history does not have any root in the United States, not even by way of the ancestors of black Americans who came from West Africa. It is an adapted Swahili word, a widely spoken language in East Africa, and full of borrowed Arabic words. Brazilians and Cubans celebrate authentic festivals to pay homage to gods from the Yoruba tribe which their ancestors brought with them on their journey across the Atlantic Ocean on the slave ship. They prayed to the gods during their journey and passed the beliefs down from generation to generation. Those gods provided them with the strength to go through the day during slavery, believing that they had some power that the slave masters didn't have, even as there was no physical proof of that power; it was all psychological. Brazilians and Cubans of all races participate in the festivals because they are authentic and represent a true history of their countries. There are a lot of traditional or historical events that took place in this country that black Americans could have picked to celebrate annually to thank God for it or remember those who made it happen. It could be the heroism or sacrifice of an individual or a platoon of black soldiers that saved the day in some battle during the Civil War. There has to be some offering that some old man or lady remembered from when the ancestors landed on this soil. How about a man like John Brown that fought and died for the freedom of the slaves based on his religious conviction? How do people allow some superficial commemoration to go on for so long where so many historic events that their forefathers lived through or celebrated exist?

It is evident that political correctness is creating new generation of Americans that will assure the country's decline. If you teach immigrants in America to be proud of a culture that did not provide them with the opportunity to live a decent life, then you are promoting the decline of America.

25. ARROGANCE OF THE ENVIRONMENTALISTS

Human civilization has now become centered on economic activities and the acquisition of material possessions. Sometimes, I can't help but wonder if modern civilization did not take a wrong turn with the invention of the automobile. To be able to get from one place to another faster, we have to extract fossil fuel that nature buried deep in the crust of the earth in a stable state, and then convert it into a state that was not what nature intended it to be. The good news is that we can develop technologies that will enable us to use resources extracted from the earth safely without jeopardizing our existence on earth.

There is no doubt that human activities in today's world are generating a lot of pollution into the atmosphere, water, and the soil. This situation can be changed for the better if all nations do their part to reduce pollution. It is in the interest of each country to take measures to reduce pollution because its population will be the first to suffer from problems caused by pollution before it reaches its neighbors. Neither the burden nor the blame should be placed on any particular nation as the current Obama administration is attempting to do with a program that resembles global restitution to underdeveloped countries by United States and some European countries. The level of excessive consumption that Obama administration believes exist in the United States also exists in the underdeveloped countries, the only difference being that the United States is doing something to control or lower pollution. In the underdeveloped countries, air pollution issues are rarely discussed, even though the inhabitants of those countries are driving almost the same type of vehicles as Americans, except that vehicles sold in the United States are equipped with sophisticated pollution control systems. Excesses are common to all human beings regardless of what society they live in. A good example is that immigrants from poor underdeveloped countries that come to the United States tend to go for expensive automobiles, especially with the easier credit system in the United States. Consider that some of these people did not even own bicycles in their countries of origin.

While environmental protection is very important, it is somewhat arrogant for proponents of environmental protection and global warming to use the word "saving the earth." What we are saving is ourselves because we are sustained by the earth; we did not create the earth. The earth existed without us and will continue to exist after us. If you compare the massive size of the earth with the area occupied by human beings, you will begin to understand how insignificant we really are to the earth. Violent demonstrations carried out by environmentalists of all kinds show that human nature does have the propensity to generate conflict. They have to vent their internal frustration on someone, and any excuse is good enough.

26. MULTI-ETHNIC SOCIETY – ADVANTAGES AND DISADVANTAGES

A multi-ethnic society could be an ideal society only if all components of it share common cultural behavior, common understanding of how the society functions, and common pride and appreciation in being part of the society. A unifying force must also exist, such as a common language, even if it is spoken with regional dialects. Brazil is a good example of a multi-ethnic society where the cultural inheritances are shared by all Brazilians, even though immigrants from all parts of the world are represented in the country. That means that regardless of whether a particular cultural activity has its root in Europe, Africa, or the native Indians, all Brazilians participate in it. Brazilians do not describe their music as black or white music and do not have the hyphenated ethnic identification such as "African-Brazilian" or "black music." The country has only one language, which is Portuguese, the language the country inherited from Portugal, the former colonizer, just the same way the United States inherited English from Great Britain.

If immigrants bring with them only the good aspects of their culture, their new society will absorb the culture and make them part of American culture. They will make America culturally richer. After all, a good thing is good no matter where it is taken to. An honest person will be respected regardless of where he or she goes. Bad cultural behavior such as Mafia organization or other types of criminal gangs brought into the United States by immigrants were not acceptable in their countries of origin and not acceptable in the United States either. Those types of cultural behaviors bring negative influence in the United States and cost the country a lot of resources to control or eradicate.

Ethnicity in the United States seemed to have taken a wrong turn earlier on in the history of the country because the races did not mix socially as an aftermath of slavery. The situation could have been different if Blacks had quickly risen once they gained their freedom to compete with Whites in all walks of life. However, when this country began to accept large number of immigrants, especially from Mexico and other third world countries, it should have looked into the future and ensured that the new immigrants are assimilated by ensuring that the country has only one language that every citizen has to understand and speak, instead of the current situation where ballots are printed in countless languages, thereby creating nations within a nation. One of the most serious lacks of foresight on the part of the earlier governments of the United States was the failure to change so many Spanish names found in states that were acquired from Mexico or ceded to the United States by Mexico after the Mexican-American war.

Leaving so many Spanish names in those states has contributed to their attraction for Mexican immigrants, who now believe they have a right to be in the United States. I guess people in those days decided to keep the Spanish names as some kind of trophies or they may have sounded exotic to them, not unlike Barack Hussein Obama, the "son of a Kenyan goat-herder and an anti-American mother from Kansas."

My overall assessment is that under the current situation of nations within a nation, multi-ethnicity may eventually turn out to contribute to the down fall of the United States.

27. MINORITY CLASSIFICATION

The classification of certain groups as minorities in the United States has turned out to be another lack of foresight on the part of American leaders (politicians). I would think that a group should be classified only as minority in a society if for some reason that group found itself involuntarily in that society. However, the United States has included in its minority classification immigrants who entered the country on their own free will, including those who entered illegally. Based on that reasoning, the only legitimate minority groups in the United States should have been the descendants of the original American Indians and African slaves. The bestowing of the minority classifications on immigrants from Mexico and other Spanish-speaking countries, Asians, Middle Easterners, and immigrants from African countries has denied the Native Americans and black Americans the full benefits they deserve due to historical indignity they suffered. They now share the benefits with people who left their countries of birth voluntarily and came to the United States to seek a better life. It would have been quite appropriate for Native Americans and black Americans to demand that the Federal Government pass a law preventing any groups that voluntarily entered this country as immigrants from being classified as minority by any state in the Union. Unfortunately, black Americans seem more focused on blaming Whites for everything that happen and didn't happen in their lives, and turn a blind eye to real present and future dangers to their political and economic survival.

I see a parallel to the behavior of black Americans to tribal situation in African countries as well as religious problems in Muslim countries. In African countries, even though tribalism occasionally erupts in murderous rampage, it does not invoke emotional feeling of helplessness as in the case of racial protests in the United States. Tribal rivalry is like a game of sports where losing a match does not mean that you will lose all future matches. The same parallel can be drawn for sectarian violence in Muslim countries. No conclusion is drawn that members of one tribe or sectarian group is intellectually superior to the other. As far as they are concerned, losing a fight does not mean that the losing side will always lose in future confrontations. They see losing as just a bad day and hope that they could win next time with better planning. That doesn't seem to be the case with racism in the United States where it has become a strong emotional issue. The emotions expressed by minorities protesting against racism show an underlining feeling of defeatism. There seems to be no feeling that they could retreat to the drawing board and come up with better plans that will help them compete or do better next time around. There seem to be a feeling of helplessness that they can't compete and win no matter how much they try. The reason is that either nature didn't provide them with the tools to compete as equals or they may have the tools but there isn't that inner energy that combines discipline, sacrifice, and perseverance to push people to achieve great things. Contrary to the strong emotion against White racism, Blacks subconsciously see Hispanics just as another tribe and, therefore, do not feel intellectually intimidated by them. They see Hispanics as being in the same boat as Blacks, so to say. That may account for their apparent lack of concern about large scale immigration, legal or illegal.

28. THE FUTURE OF AMERICA

It is my belief that United States may eventually break up into two or more countries. Many factors are already signaling the direction the country is heading. One is that the country is now permanently and irreconcilably divided into two ideological camps. It is a matter of time now before everyone gets tired of the bickering and tug-of-war and decides to seek some arrangement that will resemble a very loose federation or complete breakup as a way of avoiding a bloody civil war. After all, those kinds of things sometimes come in cycles. It's been a while since the last civil war, and the new generation of Americans doesn't have any memory of it because they didn't live through it and have no idea what it felt like for those who lived it. Secondly, the present level of uncontrollable immigration has created cultural incoherence, which brought with it the type of political corruption only seen in the third world countries. Thirdly, the nation is in a terrible debt that will not allow it to return to its former economic status. And last but not the least, too many people have been enticed into dependency on the government, which has now created a real danger of serious upheavals in the near future should the country run out of fund to maintain the free handouts.

Even if the country manages to stay intact, there is a possibility that it may end up as a mediocre society that would be somewhere between a first and third world. The reason is that it will reach a point where its population will be overwhelmed by Hispanics, with major control of political decisions. Even though Hispanics may be born and raised in the United States, they have not established any evidence of ability to create well developed and well managed societies. A good example is Mexico, which has existed side-by-side with the United States and Canada for centuries, and is endowed with a lot of natural resources, yet Mexicans are unable to develop their country to the same level as United States and Canada. Those who run Mexico are highly educated and not a bunch of ignorant politicians; yet, they have been unable to move Mexico forward. Does it make sense then for the same people to cross the border into the United States and suddenly become transformed into highly skilled governors, administrators, and clean politicians? It takes more than being born in a country to acquire the ability to create and manage a developed society. Whether the Hispanics serve as council members, city mayors, state law makers, or governors, I believe that many of them originally entered politics with the sole motivation of protest on behalf of Hispanics, rather than a conscious desire to make contributions to help the United States remain a prosperous country. Without any doubt, the United States cannot remain a prosperous country if problems of other countries are dumped into it relentlessly. In spite of these undeniable facts, the decline of the United States due to gradual power take over by Hispanics is inevitable. It's the fate of the country unless Americans are willing to face a lot of bloodshed to prevent it, and even with such a horrible bloodshed, the country will never be the same. So, it may not be a worthwhile sacrifice.

I imagine that upon break up, four new countries may emerge from the present United States. The new countries will have majority Whites, Blacks, Hispanics, and Asians respectively. It wouldn't be hard to guess which citizens of the new countries will soon start crossing the borders into other countries to seek a better life because the country they live in is poorly administered and unsafe.

29. A FINAL LOOK BACK

America is, without any doubt, a declining civilization. That decline is camouflaged by the country's technological advance, economic power, and perceived military power. The root of America's decline can be traced to exactly the same factors that make it seem great, which are affluence, the pursuit of happiness, and, of course, pleasure. But those are the same factors that cause a society to become complacent and make it ignore threats. Americans have come to believe that peace can be bought. I suspect that money played a role in the success of General Petraeus' surge in the Iraqi war by paying local leaders to turn against Al Qaeda. This policy has been practiced for many years domestically and in the Israeli-Palestinian conflict. When minorities riot or create a crime wave, or when minority activists complain about discrimination or racism, justifiably or not, money is doled out by government or private companies to pacify them, rather than reject their unreasonable demands. Minority complaints have done more than any other contributing factor to render law enforcement less effective in this country. Sometimes, you can't help but wonder if the so-called minorities would not be concerned about crime, if they were to carve their own states out of the United States.

We can no longer win a war, at least, none decisively since World War II because we have become too civilized and too sensitive to stand up for what we believe. Even the Pentagon that is supposed to prosecute United States wars could not stand up to the ACLU when it demanded that God be not mentioned in Boy Scout events sponsored by the military. I have always wondered why the United States could go to war in foreign lands to stop people in other countries from killing one another while we have ethnic gangs killing people in this country on a daily basis.

The United States cannot secure its boarders partly for fear of offending immigrants and partly because of economic expansion, even though it is not in the best interest of this country to have too many immigrants come in within a short time. Immigrants who come to live here are no longer required to adjust to American way of doing things or culture. Political correctness has labeled that a cultural discrimination. The result is that immigrants are transplanting the cultures that did not work in their lands of birth into the United States. Many of these cultures breed corruption, mismanagement, and inefficiency. Overtime the corrupt behaviors have taken root in the United States. With several nations within this nation, there is bound to be internal crises, if something serious goes wrong with the economy. A racial incident can erupt into a social strife throughout the country. Even without that happening, the rapid population growth from the uncontrolled immigration will increase friction among the different ethnic groups.

Nothing could highlight the complacency that is now causing the decline of America more than the fact that few Muslim terrorists hijacked three airplanes full of passengers, with only knives and forks. But except for one plane, the passengers made no attempt to fight the hijackers in a plane full of carryon luggage that could have been used as attack or defensive weapons against people carrying forks and knives. Also, consider that most commercial pilots came from the United States military, which means they were trained in self-defense or hand-to-hand combat, and could have been able to fight people who attacked them with forks and knives. But before you assume any blame for the passengers or the crew members, remember that we have been constantly advised by experts for many years that if you don't react against a criminal, you have a chance of getting home safely to your family. If people have been paying attention to the years of Muslim terrorist attacks, they would have realized that the Muslim terrorists only conduct suicide operations with no intention of negotiation. That was something that our experts never included in that advice about not reacting against criminals and hostage takers.

In spite of the Second Amendment, you have more people now in this country clamoring for gun control because in their mind, if all guns are banned, the criminals won't be able to kill people during the commission of crimes. But it's just another form of complacency because complacent people see no danger and don't even want to think about it.

For more than two decades, Americans and American interests have been attacked by young Arabs Muslims. One would have thought that the State Department would be more restrictive in issuing visa to young Muslims to enter the United States. Instead, American policy makers continued to allow students from the Middle Eastern countries like Iran, Saudi Arabia, Kuwait, Palestine, etc, to pour into American universities with the belief that they would become westernized and friendlier towards the West after studying in American schools. Some of those students were involved in the American Embassy seizure in Iran, and some are in the anti-American Iranian government today. The worst is that all we have succeeded in doing was teach those people how they could make bombs that they are now using against the United States.

The 9-11 hijackers were given visas during the Clinton administration to enter the United States to learn how to fly airplanes. It appears to me that this country has been shooting itself on the foot without realizing it, even as we fight war against terrorists in so many places. This country may continue to appease in order to satisfy political correctness until it is too late to effectively defend itself when it becomes obvious that the appeasement didn't work.

Unskilled immigrants generally cannot pay for an apartment in the United States, so they tend to crowd a lot of people together in a small space. That is the only way they can save money to send back to relatives in their home countries. Illegal immigrants coming across the Mexican border do not go through any kind of medical examination to determine if they are carrying any contagious disease. If it is so vital for Mexicans to cross the border into the United States for survival, and Americans see the presence of the Mexican workers as vital for the country's economic growth, then why can't the two countries get together and explore the possibility of forming a federation? This may sound like a terrible idea, but look at what has been going on gradually: Mexicans enter the United States illegally to work, some years down the road they request amnesty and receive it. For every person that receives amnesty, at least, four or more relatives follow within five to seven years, not counting the United States-born children of the amnesty recipients. Remember that Mexicans have a higher birth rate than Americans of all races. Many Mexicans are taking advantage of the law that makes every child born in the United States an automatic citizen to come across the border and have babies. As if that isn't bad enough, such babies are entitled to benefits under some children's nutritional program. Once the children reach the age of 18, they can legally bring their parents to the United States as legal immigrants, and any sibling that is 23 years or less can tag along with their parents. Political correctness strongly supported by the Democratic Party has prevented any attempt to change the law which was originally established for black Americans at the end of slavery.

The result is that the border-states of the United States are being colonized or repopulated by Mexicans, and at this point, the trend cannot be reversed. It is similar to the history of Kosovo, in the former Republic of Yugoslavia. That was where the United States went on bombing raid, under Bill Clinton, to save immigrant Muslim Albanians from the Serbs who wanted to drive them back to their country of origin. I cannot see Americans trying to send Mexicans back to Mexico, not even the ones that are here illegally. If they try, they need all the good luck they can get. America's journey down the abyss will continue.

Whether they are anti-war or not, many Americans do not seem to understand or want to understand the nature of human beings and the reasons for 9-11. First, you need to look closely at reactions of people all over the world to 9-11. Only in very few countries did we see true sympathy, without any reservation, for what happened. Most viewed the mass killing at the World Trade Center with a mute feeling that America deserved it and some, especially in the Arab countries, rejoiced openly. Why were the majority of the people in the world not sympathetic with America? It has very little to do with American policies around the world, even though those who were not bashful about giving an open opinion claimed so, but it has a lot to do with human envy. America is the country that every other country wants to be like but cannot. America's domination of the world was not intentionally planned but very much coincidental. However, people cannot rationalize about how America got to where it was, even as it has never been a colonial power. All they see is the wealth and power of America, its domination in technology, culture, and the art of filmmaking. American films and TV shows are syndicated all over the world and American music can be heard in radio stations, clubs, restaurants, and shops all over the world. Even in countries where people may not want to have anything to do with a black man, they still listen to black American music because it is American. The black American music is not superior to the music played in the Congo, Brazil, or Cuba, all of which share the same root, but it is the black American music that enjoys more worldwide audience and sales. In any international competition, such as the Olympic Games, Americans always won more medals than any other country. In almost all fields of human endeavor, Americans seem to excel, and it appears that no other country can catch up with the United States of America. It is no surprise that America's success makes other people feel smaller, even though Americans do not go out of their way to purposely intimidate others.

America's economic success and military power have created the attitude of complacency in Americans. This complacency is responsible for the United States not taking several terrorist attacks in the past seriously until 9-11. If someone hit you to get your attention, and you paid no attention, he will hit harder next time. This was the situation with the terrorists. Every time they attacked a United States target, nobody paid them serious attention, so they escalated the attack to 9-11. The same thing happens in foreign medias. The United States government makes no efforts to respond to false and malicious reports and articles and comments against it in foreign news medias. The result is that the false reports and articles become the truth to the readers. The fact that United States missions in other countries make no efforts to counter malicious lies and inaccurate reports further portrays America as arrogant. Complacent? It sure is, but not arrogant.

Every human civilized society is bound to decay somewhere along the way and eventually decline, no matter how sophisticated the society becomes. In fact, the more advanced and sophisticated the society, the more painful the decline, but the process of decay is always hard to pinpoint because it is a gradual process and often masks itself as progress. Part of being human is that we tend to get tired, bored, or simply lose interest in whatever we are doing after certain time or after doing the same things for a long period of time. Besides, we have a life span, and in spite of the history that are written for the coming generations to read and learn, things do change along the way to distort the perception of the new generation and make them unable to see that society is declining. The process of decline invariably follows the same pattern and circumstances as the ones history has taught us.

In the Roman Empire, there were lots of people coming into Rome seeking work in the construction projects at the time. In today's Western societies, the same thing has been happening ever since the industrial revolution began. The West saw immigration as positive because it brought in cheap labor for the industries and large number of consumers for the manufactured goods. But what the West could not foresee is the effect of allowing into its societies large number of immigrants from parts of the world that have been unable to move their own societies forward. Somehow, the West believed that by living in developed societies, the immigrants and their offspring would adapt to the Western way of thinking and doing things.

That again brings us back to nature and how it sets things up. To assume that immigrants from parts of the world that have been unable to develop economically and politically would be able to run developed Western societies as the Westerners could, is to say that everything in nature is equal. If everything in nature is equal, all trees would grow to the same height, if planted on the same soil, and would bear the same number of fruits, and the fruits would all be of the same size. Equality is only a human idealism; it is not supported by nature. If citizens of the so-called third world countries that immigrate to Western European countries and the United States could develop their countries, those countries would not carry the "third world" label, and the immigrants would not be leaving their homelands to look for better life elsewhere. Why the West believes that these immigrants are what it needs to keep its society going puzzles me.

The most surprising thing to me is that all the Western social scientists seem to have not only become blind to this issue but have suffered what I would like to call "politically corrected minds." That means that asking academic questions on such a serious issue as why is it that you have three countries side by side in North America, two of them are very much alike in cultural, economic, and political developments, but the third is totally different would be considered politically incorrect. Whose fault is it that such a situation exists? Does it have anything to do with the type of people that administer the societies? I have always heard the expression about the citizens of a country being a good people but just have a bad government. I disagree strongly with this expression because I believe that every society deserves the kind of government it has, if not, the government would not exist. In countries that hold democratic election for their governments, the people are responsible for who they put in office. If they cannot elect good people to office, for whatever reasons, they have themselves to blame. Besides, the mentality with which the people in office run the country is a product of that society.

30. AS YOU GO THROUGH THE DAY

Remember that:

1.   Life is so uncertain that, in the end, what counts is how you lived.

2.   Life makes sense as long as the reasons for our existence are defined.

3.   The search for the absolute truth about life leads through a circular path.

4.   We may discover what we didn't know but may never know how much we still don't know.

5.   You can only see yourself through others.

6.   You should always think "Details" and not "Big"; "Detail" is the building block of all knowledge.

7.   If you never show others that you don't like them, they will never blame you for it.

8.   Life is painful, and it is a challenge to all human beings to make it as less painful as possible.

9.   In a way, life could have been amusing, if we weren't aware of our existence.

10.   The most frustrating thing about the awareness of our existence is that it gives us the ability to ask questions but not to answer them.

11.   The rich and the intellectuals may feel immune to unacceptable behaviors of some members of the society, but their lack of concern will eventually cause the erosion of the democratic systems.

12.   There are always other people who live around you, use the same roadway, head in the same destination as you are going, which shows that your thing is everybody's thing.

13.   We will never know what being satisfied with everything about life may do to a person, since we will never meet such a person.

14.   Freedom misleads the poor and the ignorant; oppression makes heroes out of them.

15. Our activities on earth may lead to the extinction of humans, and when we are all gone, there will be nobody to tell or be told about our lives.

16. If you make the physical world a happy one for yourself and others, chances are that your spiritual life or the life after will follow suit.

17. A civilized person must learn to pass on good experiences and discard the bad ones.

18. Emancipation is a self-process; declaration of freedom is only a signal to start the process.

19. You should neither exploit nor blame others because of attributes bestowed on you by nature.

20. Relativity in human experience means that the behaviors of one person can mark him out as good or bad when compared against others.

21. Poverty is not lack of material wealth but of ability to use available resources.

22. You must judge others with the same logic with which you judge yourself.

23. Nature imposed certain limitations on us all, and only with conscious efforts can such limitations be overcome.

24. A song tells us nothing about how it is danced; the singer makes up the dance.

25. You may wait forever to meet a person who likes others who do not like him or her.

26. Inequality is not the result of perfection of any particular group of people but of failure of the other group to produce equal results.

27. Many of us lie and cheat to get ahead; yet we hope to pass on a just world to those that come after us.

28. Some people use poverty, as an excuse to perpetuate bad behaviors and it is frightening to find out what they might do, if they become wealthy and powerful.

29. Any protest is counterproductive if it results in today's protester becoming tomorrow's perpetrator of the same injustice to others.

30. Self-evaluation, in relation to other individuals and groups, should be based not on the faults of others or wrong they have done, but on the useful contributions they have made and the good they have done.

31. Population explosion may provide businesses and industries with cheap labor and consumers, but effectively guarantees future chaos in society.

32. Others cannot make you truly equal to them; you have to make yourself truly equal to others.

33.	Always remember that the world will go on without you, no matter how smart you may be.

34.	An affluent society exposes the commonality of human greed.

35.	The little that we do, be it good or bad has some influence on others around us.

36.	Our present civilization was created from philosophy; if we abandon philosophy, we will fall back to where we started.

37.	We have seen a tremendous technological progress in this millennium; now the challenge for the next millennium will be to match technological progress with equal improvement in human character.

38.	A society may have collective civilization but individuals within that society may not be civilized.

39.	Those who make no efforts to help themselves deserve no helps from others.

40.	People are often looking outside for something that is within them.

31. A PESSIMIST'S PRESCRIPTION FOR LONGEVITY

➢	Accept life as an unknown event whose end is certain but unpredictable.

➢	Believe that you are a good person deep down, even if you are not rich and famous.

- Be principled and live by defined do's and don'ts or right and wrong.

- Maintain a balance in your life and avoid the seesaw type of behavior.

- Don't expect people to do for you what you cannot do for yourself.

- Expect people to ignore you when they need nothing from you.

- Expect people to ignore your point of view, if it will cause them to do some hard thinking.

- Expect people to talk more about your faults than about your good qualities.

- Expect to be called and treated as an odd-man-out for not accepting a fad.

- Expect to gain more friends if you suddenly come into fortune.

- Don't expect people to treat you the way they would like to be treated.

- Expect people to lie when it is in their best interest.

- Expect people to come up with clever arguments to support their behavior or action.

- Expect people to always act in their own best interest, not yours.

- Expect people to act more out of instinct than out of logic.

- Expect people to be more driven by material gains than by philosophical considerations.

- Expect people to tell you their story rather than listen to yours.

An Essay by an Optimistic Pessimist

- Expect people to prefer a different version or color of whatever you have just bought.

- Don't expect everyone that talks and acts nice to be necessarily dependable.

- Don't expect people to obey the rules, unless there is some penalty for violating them.

- Don't expect every driver on the roadway to know or do what he or she is supposed to do.

- Don't go with the crowd if you believe the crowd is going in the wrong direction.

- Don't rely on prayers to get things done, just do what you are supposed to do.

- Realize that life requires more sacrifices than benefits.

- Realize that moments of happiness in life are very few.

- If you hope to accomplish something on the basis of luck, be prepared for the opposite result.

- Don't expect free-flowing traffic when you are in a hurry.

- Don't always expect the person or thing you believe in and defend to prove you right.

- Expect unwanted color to turn permanent after fading into your best apparel.

- Even as you are not what you wanted to be, you may have to accept that that is all you can be.